# FORERUNNERS

## OF THE

# FAITH

FOREWORD BY JOHN MACARTHUR

# FORERUNNERS
## OF THE
# FAITH

### 13 LESSONS TO UNDERSTAND AND APPRECIATE
### THE BASICS OF CHURCH HISTORY

TEACHER'S
GUIDE

# NATHAN BUSENITZ

MOODY PUBLISHERS
CHICAGO

Interior Design: Smartt Guys design
Cover Design: Kaylee Lockenour

All websites and phone numbers listed herein are accurate at the time of publication but may change in the future or cease to exist. The listing of website references and resources does not imply publisher endorsement of the site's entire contents. Groups and organizations are listed for informational purposes, and listing does not imply publisher endorsement of their activities.

ISBN: 978-0-8024-1977-4

Originally delivered by fleets of horse-drawn wagons, the affordable paperbacks from D. L. Moody's publishing house resourced the church and served everyday people. Now, after more than 125 years of publishing and ministry, Moody Publishers' mission remains the same—even if our delivery systems have changed a bit. For more information on other books (and resources) created from a biblical perspective, go to: www.moodypublishers.com or write to:

Moody Publishers
820 N. LaSalle Boulevard
Chicago, IL 60610

1 3 5 7 9 10 8 6 4 2

*Printed in the United States of America*

# CONTENTS

# FOREWORD

*By John MacArthur*

Church history begins and ends with Jesus Christ. From start to finish, the church age is bookended by His first and second comings. Our Lord's ascension to heaven and the sending of His Spirit at Pentecost mark the beginnings of church history; His return for His bride will bring the church age to a close.

The Lord Jesus not only defines the scope of church history, but He is the supreme focus of every part of it. Christ is the Head of the church and the Lord of history. Thus, both the church and its history exist to magnify His glory. One day, the church on earth will be gathered in heaven, and time itself will be wrapped up in eternity. Church history will be no more. But the doxological purpose for which it was ordained will endure forever, as glorified saints from every tribe and tongue lift their voices in endless praise to the Lamb.

A survey of church history, properly framed, fixes the focus on the Lord Jesus. It puts our eyes on Him (Heb. 12:2). History bears witness to both His work and His Word, and it generates genuine worship as a result. We see the truth of Christ's saving work, in generation after generation, radically transform lives through the power of the gospel. We see the authority of His Word repeatedly triumph over heretical errors and empty philosophies, as it governs the belief and practice of the redeemed. We also see the resounding response, as His people rejoin in praise and thanksgiving. The halls of church history reverberate with the worship of the redeemed, from the days of the apostles to the present.

*Forerunners of the Faith* provides an engaging and accessible introduction to church history. But it does far more than merely present information in a clear and simple way. Armed with a biblical lens, *Forerunners* lifts the eyes of its readers beyond the events and figures of the past. It places the focus on the Lord Jesus—on His work, His Word, and the worship He deserves. Whether you embark on this journey of discovery by yourself or as part of a group, you are sure to come away with a greater sense of awe and wonder for all the Lord has done through the centuries to build His church.

Far too many believers today remain ignorant about their history as members of the body of Christ. Some may be indifferent, unaware of the faithful examples and important lessons waiting to be discovered. Others are intimidated, fearful that the subject may expose them to error and confusion. *Forerunners of the Faith* cuts through the fog with biblical clarity and practical relevance. Whether you are new to the subject or simply eager to refresh your appreciation for the richness of your Christian heritage, you've come to the right place. A compelling and Christ-exalting journey awaits you on the pages that follow.

# HOW TO USE THIS MANUAL

*Tips for Preparing and Presenting the Material*

## FOR THE TEACHER

*Forerunners of the Faith* is a curriculum designed to introduce believers to the rich heritage of the historical church. It is designed to focus on key figures in church history while also providing a basic framework for understanding significant events and developments.

Students are expected to fill out their Student Workbook while listening to you present the material to them. The material they need to complete their workbook is found in this Teacher's Edition manual.

Being an effective teacher involves both careful preparation and clear presentation. Here are some helpful tips for maximizing your effectiveness in both of those areas.

### Careful Preparation

Proper planning and preparation are critical to effective teaching. The Teacher's Edition of this workbook provides you with a clear lesson plan to follow. The curriculum is designed for a single lesson to be completed each week.

Start by downloading and listening to the corresponding lecture from **www.tms.edu/forerunners**. These **audio lessons** will go into much more detail and nuance than can be accomplished in the limited format of this workbook. Follow along in this Teacher's Edition manual, and take notes as needed.

Read the discussion questions. Use your Bible to formulate an answer. It is important to show your students throughout these lessons that the Bible, not church history, is the believer's ultimate authority.

Come to class with a firm grasp of the material. You will use the material in this Teacher's Edition manual as your lecture notes. It is intended to provide you with the structure and talking points needed to present the material. It also corresponds to the workbooks your students will use during the class.

### Clear Presentation

Manage your time well. Each lesson is designed for an hour-long class period, but can be adapted for other lengths of time. It is important for you, the teacher, to manage the time carefully so the lesson is paced appropriately.

Be familiar with the material. This familiarity will enable you to maintain eye contact and exhibit freedom in presenting the content.

Expand on the notes. The printed notes are not intended merely to be read verbatim. Rather, they are designed as talking points. By listening to the lecture and preparing carefully for your lesson, you will be able to expand beyond what is printed in this manual.

Engage with student questions. Allow your students to ask questions, and be willing to dialogue with them about the material. If you do not know the answer to a question, be honest and let them know you will investigate their question and try to answer it at a later time. (You can also encourage them to investigate and report on their findings at the next class.)

> For questions that involve theological or moral issues, be sure to use God's Word in your answer. As noted above, it is important to demonstrate that Scripture, not church history, is the believer's authority.

Have fun. Your students' attitudes toward the material will likely reflect your own. If you demonstrate enthusiasm for church history, that excitement will be contagious. It will also make your class time far more effective.

### *Going Above and Beyond*

Some teachers may want to dig deeper into their study of church history, beyond what is included in this concise manual. While resources on the internet are abundant and often free, they are not always trustworthy. Here are a few recommended resources:

> Nick Needham, 2000 Years of Christ's Power, 4 vols. (Christian Focus)

> Sinclair Ferguson, In the Year of Our Lord (Reformation Trust)

> Earl Cairns, Christianity through the Centuries (Zondervan)

> Stephen Nichols, Five Minutes in Church History Podcast
https://www.5minutesinchurchhistory.com/

> Robert Godfrey, A Survey of Church History (Ligonier Ministries)

# INTRODUCTION

## WHY STUDY CHURCH HISTORY?
*Reasons Every Christian Should Care about the Past*

### I. INTRODUCTION

As a church history professor, I routinely face the challenge of engaging students in a subject that may initially seem either unfamiliar or uninteresting. Despite the misconceptions, church history is neither boring nor irrelevant. It is so much more than names, dates, timelines, and charts.

Some students start out thinking, *I hate history.* Maybe so, but the study of church history is not primarily about *history*. It's about *the church*, the bride of Christ, the most precious institution on earth. It's about what God has been doing in the world for the last two thousand years. And that means it should matter to every believer.

Others might wonder why they should study church history if our primary focus ought to be on studying *the Bible.* Without question, the Christian's daily spiritual diet should consist of the pure milk of the Word (1 Peter 2:1–3). Nonetheless, the study of church history is a rich and profitable exercise. It can never replace the study of Scripture, but it can enrich it, as you learn from prior generations of believers who faithfully studied and applied biblical truth.

To be clear, the Word of God is the final authority over church history. But the study of church history, when evaluated through the lens of Scripture, is a faith-affirming exercise. I have experienced that reality firsthand. The deeper I've investigated the history of the church, the more I have grown to appreciate the power and authority of God's Word—because I've seen that power vividly illustrated in the testimonies of past generations of believers.

It is the teacher's responsibility to convince the student of the importance and relevance of the subject being taught. When asked why church history is so important, if I only have a minute or two to answer, I usually highlight the following three points, using the acronym *ABC*.

*A* is for _____Apologetics._____ Believers today should take an interest in church history because it will help them guard against false teaching. The study of church history helps us understand how false movements arose and how believers in the past have refuted them.

*B* is for _____Biography._____ The halls of church history are filled with compelling accounts of faithful men and women who made great sacrifices to follow Christ. Their examples motivate us to walk in a manner worthy of the gospel.

*C* is for _____Curiosity._____ The study of church history answers many questions and shows us important connections. It explains how broader Christendom came to be what it is today. How did certain practices or movements develop? Why are things the way they are? Church history helps us find answers to those lines of inquiry.

## II. TEN REASONS TO STUDY CHURCH HISTORY[1]

When given a bit more time to answer the question, "Why is church history important?", we can list ten reasons. These represent an expansion of the three points listed above.

1. **Studying church history is important because most contemporary Christians don't know much about it. But they should.**

   Sadly, most contemporary evangelicals know very little about the history of Christianity. Even in Reformed circles, an understanding of church history often goes back to only the Reformation. But the history of the gospel spans all the way back to the New Testament.

   If your knowledge of church history jumps from the apostle John (on Patmos) to Martin Luther (in Wittenberg), with little to nothing in between, you ought to consider filling in the gaps. The 1,500 years between Pentecost and the Reformation include many significant people—fellow believers and faithful leaders—whom God used in strategic ways to advance His kingdom purposes.

   Evangelical church history—all 2,000 years of it—is a goldmine of theological treasure. In their attempts to juvenilize the church, many evangelical congregations spurn history as if it were outdated and unimportant. We do ourselves a great disservice if we choose to remain ignorant.

   Does God consider history to be important? Certainly He does. Though it is not church history, God used Israel's history to teach them spiritual truths throughout the Old Testament (see Deut. 6:21–25). And in the New Testament, the Holy Spirit saw fit to inspire a book of church history, starting from the Day of Pentecost and running through Paul's first Roman imprisonment.

   While the inspired record of church history ends with the book of Acts, Christians are blessed to have wonderful resources that detail the history of the church from the first century to the present. Those who ignore the profound riches of their own spiritual heritage don't know what they are missing—namely, the life-changing opportunity to be challenged, instructed, and encouraged in the faith by those who've gone before us.

2. **Because God is at work in history. Equally, history is a testimony to God's sovereign providence.**

   Pardon the cliché, but it really is *His story*. Everything is working according to His plans, and He is orchestrating all of it for His eternal glory (see 1 Cor. 15:20–28). God declares Himself to be the Lord of history:

   > **Isaiah 46:9–10**—"Remember the former things long past, for I am God, and there is no other; I am God, and there is no one like Me, declaring the end from the beginning, and from ancient times things which have not been done, saying, 'My purpose will be established, and I will accomplish all My good pleasure.'"

   Studying church history reminds us that our God is on His throne. He reigns. He is perfectly accomplishing His purposes and providentially preserving His people and His truth in every generation. No matter how immoral or antagonistic toward God society becomes, we already know how history ends. What comfort there is in remembering that the Lord of history is working all things together for His glory and our good.

   One of the greatest theological lessons any believer can learn is to rest in the sovereignty of God. The Scriptures are filled with examples of men and women who trusted God and acted upon their faith in Him (see Heb. 11). Church history, likewise, consists of wonderful examples of faithful Christians whose lives are testimonies to the providential care of their heavenly Father.

3. **Because the Lord Jesus said He would build His church. To study church history is to watch His promise unfold.**

   In **Matthew 16:15–18**, we read,

   > [Jesus] said to them, "But who do you say that I am?" Simon Peter answered, "You are the Christ, the Son of the living God." And Jesus said to him, "Blessed are you, Simon Barjona, because flesh and blood did not reveal this to you, but My Father who is in heaven. I also say to you that you are Peter, and upon this rock I will build My church; and the gates of Hades will not overpower it."

   The church is established on the gospel truth that Jesus is the Christ, the Son of the living God. The church's unconquerable history is evidence that He is indeed who He claimed to be.

   The church is the only institution that Jesus ever established. That alone is reason enough to study church history. Moreover, His promise—that the gates of hell will never overpower the church—gives us reason to hope even when the church appears to be weak and infirm. Christ's promise keeps us optimistic, because our hope is in Him and not in the things of this world.

   When we study church history, we are reminded of those times when the gates of hell appeared ominous and threatening, and yet the church survived and prevailed through God's power. When courageous Christians were severely persecuted to the point of death for the sake of the truth; or when Arianism threatened to overrun the Roman Empire and Athanasius stood, seemingly alone, against the world; or when the sacramental system of the late-medieval church threatened to eclipse the gospel of grace; or when liberal theology infiltrated the universities of nineteenth- and twentieth-century Western society . . .

   These and countless other examples embolden us to face today's challenges and persecutions with the confidence of knowing that we belong to a cause that cannot fail.

4. **Because church history is our history. As believers, we are members of the body of Christ, and part of the bride of Christ.**

   When we study the history of the church, we are not merely studying people, places, and events. We are studying the history of Christ's bride. If we belong to Christ, then we, too, are part of that bride. As Paul explained to the Ephesians,

   > **Ephesians 5:25–27**—"Husbands, love your wives, just as Christ also loved the church and gave Himself up for her, so that He might sanctify her, having cleansed her by the washing of water with the word, that He might present to Himself the church in all her glory, having no spot or wrinkle or any such thing; but that she would be holy and blameless."

   When we study church history, we come to see who we are, where we've come from, and how we fit into the flow of God's kingdom work in the world. We are studying our spiritual family tree. The Lord Jesus Himself cares deeply about His bride (see Rev. 1–3), and we should, too.

   On a practical note, one of the great ways to remind ourselves that we are part of a body of believers that spans the centuries is through singing hymns. When we sing hymns like *Be Thou My Vision* (a sixth-century Irish hymn) or *O Sacred Head Now Wounded* (penned by either Bernard of Clairvaux in the twelfth century or Arnulf of Louvain in the thirteenth) or *A Mighty Fortress* (written by Martin Luther in the sixteenth century), we connect ourselves to the history of the church.

   Knowing the history behind the hymns reminds us that we belong to the corporate body of believers, the universal church. Just as we have brothers and sisters across the world, we also have brothers and sisters from generations past who are now in heaven rejoicing around Christ's throne. The study of church history allows us to meet them, as it were, as we read their testimonies and learn about their lives. It also reminds us that one day soon we will go to join with them in eternal praise, when we see our Savior face to face.

Studying the history of the church reminds us that we are part of something bigger than ourselves, our own local congregations, or even the century in which we live. We are part of the bride of Christ—and His bride consists of all the redeemed from every generation.

5. **Because sound doctrine has been guarded and passed down by faithful generations throughout history.**

In **2 Timothy 2:2**, Paul told his son in the faith, "The things which you have heard from me in the presence of many witnesses, entrust these to faithful men who will be able to teach others also." To study church history is to meet the generations of Christians who loved biblical truth and faithfully passed it on to those who came after. Moreover, it is encouraging to know that the truths we hold dear have been cherished by believers all the way back to the time of the apostles.

The study of church history reminds us that we are standing on the shoulders of those who have come before us. The halls of history are filled with accounts of those who loved the truth and fought valiantly to preserve it. Thus, while we recognize that church history is not authoritative (only Scripture is), we are wise to glean from the wisdom of past church leaders, theologians, and pastors. Their creeds, commentaries, and sermons represent lifetimes of meditating on the text and walking with God. We would be unwise to ignore their voices and their insights—as we similarly seek to rightly divide the Word.

Further, when we study church history, we are reminded that some truths are worth fighting (and dying) for. We remember that we are part of something bigger than ourselves. And like those who have come before us, we too have a responsibility to faithfully guard the treasure of biblical truth and sound doctrine that has been entrusted to us, being careful to pass it on to those who will follow us.

6. **Because, just as we are encouraged by the history of truth, we are also warned by the history of error. This enables us to be equipped as apologists.**

The New Testament is full of warnings about false teaching, both refuting it in the first century and warning that it would come in the centuries that followed (Acts 20:28–30; 1 Tim. 4:1). When we study church history, we learn not only the history of the truth but also the history of error. We see where heresies and the cults originated, and we have the benefit of seeing orthodoxy defended and the truth being preserved.

The New Testament calls all Christians to be able to defend the faith. In the words of 1 Peter 3:15, "Sanctify Christ as Lord in your hearts, always being ready to make a defense to everyone who asks you to give an account for the hope that is in you, yet with gentleness and reverence." Titus 1:8–10 similarly requires that an elder must be one who holds "fast the faithful word which is in accordance with the teaching, so that he will be able both to exhort in sound doctrine and to refute those who contradict." That is a quality all believers should desire to emulate.

Any defense of the Christian faith must be founded on the Scriptures. But church history also serves as a valuable, albeit secondary, apologetic tool.

For example, knowing a little church history quickly silences silly allegations against Christianity. Knowing a little church history is especially helpful in witnessing to Muslims, Mormons, Jehovah's Witnesses, and members of other pseudo-Christian cults. Understanding church history is even helpful in defending key areas of doctrine—showing that a contemporary evangelical understanding of Scripture has not deviated from the teachings of the apostolic church.

As believers, we are commanded to be ready to give a defense for our hope. The study of church history is an ally in that cause.

7. **Because we have much to learn from those who walked with God (cf. Heb. 11).**

In Hebrews 12:1, we read of "a great cloud of witnesses"—believers in generations past whose lives give testimony to the faithfulness of God. While the author of Hebrews was specifically referring to Old Testament saints (see Heb. 11), the testimonies of all who have come before us provide a powerful encouragement to remain faithful ourselves.

Faithfulness to the Lord, to His Word, and to His people is what defines a hero of the faith. And church history offers us many such faithful men and women to choose from. Their lives should inspire, motivate, and encourage us as we run the race with endurance. Their heaven-focused perspective reminds us to keep our eyes on Christ, the Author and Perfecter of the faith. As C. S. Lewis famously said, "If you read history you will find out that the Christians who did most for the present world were precisely those who thought most of the next." Gleaning those kinds of devotional gems begins with reading church history.

Seasoned pastors often talk about identifying "mentors" from church history, faithful Christians from the past whose lives they have studied and desire to emulate. That is a practice all believers should seriously consider. In the opinion of this writer, Christian biography ought to be a staple part of any believer's regular reading diet. I highly recommend reading at least one church history biography every year. You will be greatly encouraged and inspired to continued faithfulness by that simple practice alone.

8. **Because just as we can learn from the good examples of faithful Christians (see Reason 7), we likewise have much to learn from those who failed at various points.**

It is a familiar saying, but often true: those who don't know history are doomed to repeat the mistakes of the past.

In church history, we see examples of all kinds of spiritual failure. There are those who strayed into heresy, those who gave way to corruption, those who denied the faith, and those who fell morally. The lives of such individuals serve as a warning for us.

In 1 Corinthians 10:1–13, the apostle Paul uses the negative illustration of the Israelites in the wilderness to teach his readers an important spiritual lesson. Paul's example sets a precedent for the way we think about both biblical history and church history.

We can learn powerful lessons about what to avoid from things like the influx of paganism into Roman Christianity, the corruption of the papacy, the Crusades, the development of liberalism, and so on. Learning from past failures helps guard us from repeating those same errors.

Church history is proof that spiritual failure can come rapidly with devastating results—a point illustrated in the New Testament by the Galatians, who were quickly tempted to abandon the true gospel (Gal. 1:6–9). It reminds us of the need to be vigilant—to watch our lives and our doctrine closely, so as not to fall into similar snares and pitfalls.

9. **Because studying the past helps us understand the resources, opportunities, and freedoms we enjoy in the present.**

Often, we take for granted the blessings we enjoy living in the modern age. The study of church history reminds us of the great sacrifices made and challenges faced by previous generations of believers. It increases our thankfulness for what we have, and it motivates us to be good stewards of the incredible opportunities God has afforded us.

The history of the English Bible, for example, reminds us to be thankful that we have a personal copy of God's Word in our own language. The history of persecution emboldens us in our evangelism, as we witness the faithfulness of the martyrs and recognize how unique the freedoms we enjoy really are. The history of missions makes us grateful for advancements in travel and technology, while simultaneously inspiring us to do more in our effort to reach the world for Christ.

It is also interesting, on a tangential note, to realize that our generation represents the first to really wrestle with the implications of the information age for the church. In many ways, modern technology affords us with opportunities that those of previous generations could never have imagined. But such advancements also put the onus on us to think carefully and biblically about the way we use them. We are setting the precedent for the way future generations will think about the church's interaction with technology and media.

10. **Because history gives twenty-first century Christians a right perspective about their own place in the church age.**

It is important to realize that we are part of church history. We are part of the current generation of believers, and we have a responsibility to faithfully guard the truth and pass it on to those who come after us.

Studying church history helps us recognize that we are part of something much bigger than ourselves, our local congregation, or even the evangelical movement as it exists today. The history of Christianity spans two millennia, of which we are but a momentary blip.

Studying church history also opens our eyes to the fact that every generation of believers is greatly affected by the time and culture in which they live, such that they themselves do not even realize the effects. We can then, in turn, ask ourselves what impact our culture has on our own application of biblical truth.

Finally, and most importantly, studying church history helps us remember that Christ is the Lord of the church in every age; and to remind ourselves of what a great privilege it is to minister in His service. It also motivates us to look forward to the day when He returns, and church history officially comes to its end.

## III. GETTING STARTED

Armed with reasons *why* the study of the past is important, you are now ready to embark on a journey through two thousand years of Christian history.

Please be aware that a series of thirteen lessons can only scratch the surface with regard to all that God has done over the last two millennia.

The goal of these lessons is threefold: (1) to introduce you to some of the major figures and events in church history, (2) to provide a basic historical framework for understanding church history, and (3) to encourage you in the faith by offering a glimpse into what God has done in prior generations.

# PART I

# THE
# APOSTOLIC AGE

1ST CENTURY

# THE BIBLICAL FRAMEWORK
## Identifying the Pillars of the Faith

**KEY PASSAGE: 2 Timothy 1:13–14**

*"Retain the standard of sound words which you have heard from me, in the faith and love which are in Christ Jesus. Guard, through the Holy Spirit who dwells in us, the treasure which has been entrusted to you."*

| Doctrinal Pillar 1: The Word of God | | Doctrinal Pillar 2: The Work of God | | Doctrinal Pillar 3: The Worship of God |
|---|---|---|---|---|
| | 16th–20th Centuries | | Early/Late Modern Age | |
| | 11th–15th Centuries | | High/Late Middle Ages | |
| | 6th–10th Centuries | | Early Middle Ages | |
| | 2nd–5th Centuries | | Patristic Period | |

**The Foundation: Jesus Christ and the Apostolic Witness to Him**

## I. PICTURING THE CHURCH AS A BUILDING

One of the New Testament metaphors for the church is that of a building. Jesus Himself promised to build His church, and guaranteed that it would not fail (see Matt. 16:18).

Scripture points to Christ (and the truth about Him) as the foundation on which the church is built.

**1 Corinthians 3:9–11**—"For we are God's fellow workers; you are God's field, God's building . . . . For no man can lay a foundation other than the one which is laid, which is Jesus Christ."

**Ephesians 2:19–22**—"So then you are no longer strangers and aliens, but you are fellow citizens with the saints, and are of God's household, having been built on the foundation of the apostles and prophets, Christ Jesus Himself being the corner stone, in whom the whole building, being fitted together, is growing into a holy temple in the Lord, in whom you also are being built together into a dwelling of God in the Spirit."

**1 Peter 2:4–5**—"And coming to Him as to a living stone which has been rejected by men, but is choice and precious in the sight of God, you also, as living stones, are being built up as a spiritual house."

- Peter continues in vv. 6–8 to explain that Jesus Christ is the cornerstone—the foundation stone on which the church is built.

The universal church consists of believers who have embraced the Lord Jesus in saving faith. They have built their lives on the foundation of Christ and His Word. As Jesus Himself explained in the Sermon on the Mount:

**Matthew 7:24–25**—"Therefore everyone who hears these words of Mine and acts on them, may be compared to a wise man who built his house on the rock. And the rain fell, and the floods came, and the winds blew and slammed against that house; and yet it did not fall, for it had been founded on the rock."

## II. THREE DOCTRINAL PILLARS

Following the metaphor of a building, we might ask: "What are the essential doctrinal pillars that define biblical orthodoxy and characterize the true church?"

The New Testament identifies three of these doctrinal pillars.

The true church is characterized by its commitment to:

1. __The Supremacy of the Word of God__ The true church looks to Scripture as its final authority for doctrine (what to believe) and practice (how to live). Followers of Jesus submit to Him by submitting to His Word (John 10:27).

2. __The Sufficiency of the Work of God__ The true church understands that the redemptive work of Christ accomplished everything necessary for salvation. Sinners are justified by God's grace through faith in Christ, apart from their own merits or works.

3. __The Sanctity of the Worship of God__ The true church worships the triune God (Father, Son, and Holy Spirit) in spirit (purity of devotion) and in truth (purity of doctrine). It rejects false forms of worship and repudiates anything that might distort or distract from its sincere devotion to God.

By contrast, the New Testament confronts and condemns those who would (1) undermine the authority of Scripture, or (2) add works to the gospel of grace, or (3) contaminate the undefiled worship that God requires.

In this lesson, we will develop these points from the Bible. These three pillars provide a doctrinal grid through which we can evaluate church history.

### A. The Supremacy of the Word of God

The true church embraces and submits to the Word of God.

Because Jesus is the Head of the church, His Word is the authority for His people. Paul highlighted both the authority and sufficiency of Scripture when he told Timothy:

> **2 Timothy 3:16–17**— "All Scripture is inspired by God and profitable for teaching, for reproof, for correction, for training in righteousness; so that the man of God may be adequate, equipped for every good work."

Conversely, false teachers seek to undermine the Scriptures. For example, in the book of 2 Peter, Peter denounced those who deny the Word of God by distorting its teaching or seeking to thwart its authority (2 Peter 3:16–17).

In Mark 7, Jesus made it clear the Word of God is authoritative over the traditions of men. When the Pharisees confronted Jesus because His disciples were not following the extrabiblical traditions of first-century Judaism, He rebuked them:

**Mark 7:5–13**—"The Pharisees and the scribes asked Him, 'Why do Your disciples not walk according to the tradition of the elders, but eat their bread with impure hands?' And He said to them, 'Rightly did Isaiah prophesy of you hypocrites, as it is written:

> "This people honors Me with their lips,
> But their heart is far away from Me.
> "But in vain do they worship Me,
> Teaching as doctrines the precepts of men."

Neglecting the commandment of God, you hold to the tradition of men.'

He was also saying to them, "You are experts at setting aside the commandment of God in order to keep your tradition . . . , thus invalidating the word of God by your tradition which you have handed down; and you do many things such as that.'"

As Jesus explained, the Word of God supersedes religious tradition. Scripture is the authority over tradition, not the other way around.

This is an important principle for thinking biblically about church history. As traditions begin to develop throughout the centuries, they must be evaluated through the lens of biblical truth.

❖ **For Discussion:** Read John 10:27. According to that verse, what is one of the defining marks of the followers of Jesus? How should that reality apply to the church and its relationship to the Word of Christ (Col. 3:16–17)?

### What About Apostolic Tradition?[1]

Certain segments of broader Christendom, like Roman Catholicism and Eastern Orthodoxy, elevate religious tradition to a level of authority equal to Scripture. This is because their systems include beliefs and practices not found in the Bible.

To justify their elevation of religious tradition, they point to verses in the New Testament that speak of apostolic tradition.

Those verses include the following:

**1 Corinthians 11:2**—"Now I praise you because you remember me in everything and hold firmly to the traditions, just as I delivered them to you."

**2 Thessalonians 2:15**—"So then, brethren, stand firm and hold to the traditions which you were taught, whether by word of mouth or by letter from us."

**2 Thessalonians 3:6**—"Keep away from every brother who leads an unruly life and not according to the tradition which you received from us."

While these verses mention the word "tradition," do they really justify the non-biblical traditions that developed over the centuries in church history?

To answer that question, consider the following four points:

1. The word "tradition" comes from a Greek word that means _____"that which is given over."_____
   The Latin word, *traditio*, means _____"that which is handed down,"_____ and it is from that Latin word
   that we get the English word *tradition*.

   So when we see the word "tradition" in the New Testament associated with the apostles, it is not
   referring to an elaborate liturgical system of non-biblical customs—like those found in Roman
   Catholicism or Eastern Orthodoxy today.

   Instead, it is referring to apostolic instruction that was given to the church, either through
   teaching and preaching or through writing.

   Hence, we must not read later patristic and medieval customs back into the word "tradition" in the
   New Testament. To do so would be both anachronistic and erroneous.

2. Apostolic tradition has been preserved for us in the writings of _____the New Testament._____
   When we read the New Testament, we find exactly what the apostles taught.

   We do not need to wonder about the content of apostolic tradition, because it is recorded for us on
   the pages of Scripture.

   When we evaluate extrabiblical tradition in light of the New Testament, we are bringing the
   authoritative instruction of Christ and the apostles to bear on that tradition.

   We are right to evaluate anything that claims to be apostolic or authoritative against the standard
   of what we know to be apostolic and authoritative. Said another way, we ought to evaluate
   extrabiblical tradition against the standard of Scripture.

3. Believers are instructed, by the New Testament, to evaluate all teachings and traditions in light of
   _____God's Word._____

   The New Testament repeatedly warns the church about the threat of false teachers.

   Paul urged the Thessalonians (in 1 Thess. 5:21) to "examine everything carefully."

   He issued a similar warning in Colossians 2:8:

   > **Colossians 2:8**—"See to it that no one takes you captive through philosophy
   > and empty deception, according to the tradition of men."

   We avoid the errors of false teaching and heretical traditions by carefully examining everything
   according to the standard of divine truth—the Word of God.

   In 2 Timothy 3:16–17, Paul's statement about the inspiration and sufficiency of Scripture comes
   after his warning about false teachers. What is the antidote to false teaching? The Word of God.

   Believers can differentiate between truth and falsehood by evaluating it in light of the Scriptures.

   Even the apostle Paul invited that kind of scrutiny. That is why Luke can say of the Bereans, who
   heard the teachings of Paul, that they were "more noble-minded than those in Thessalonica, for
   they received the word with great eagerness, examining the Scriptures daily to see whether these
   things were so" (Acts 17:11).

Though he was an apostle, Paul welcomed the Bereans' eagerness to test the veracity of his teaching against the standard of written revelation.

When we evaluate extrabiblical traditions through the lens of Scripture, we are doing exactly what the apostles themselves tell us to do in the New Testament: to examine everything carefully and do so by searching the Scriptures.

Thus, we can safely say that any tradition that fails to measure up to Scripture's standard is neither apostolic nor authoritative.

4. The early church viewed the writings of the apostles as inherently _____authoritative._____ They understood that any non-biblical traditions must be evaluated against the standard of Scripture.

Many examples from early church history could be given to illustrate this point. Consider the following two:

> **Irenaeus (c. 130–202):** "We have learned from none others the plan of our salvation, than from those through whom the Gospel has come down to us [that's a reference to the apostles], which they did at one time proclaim in public, and, at a later period, by the will of God, handed down to us [a verb form of the word 'tradition'] in the Scriptures, to be the ground and pillar of our faith."[2]

Irenaeus recognized that what the apostles taught orally, they handed down to the church in the writings of Scripture.

A century and a half later, Basil of Caesarea talks about his theological battles against the followers of Arius—a false teacher who denied the deity of Christ. Notice what Basil says:

> **Basil (330–379):** "I do not consider it fair that the custom [or tradition] which obtains among them should be regarded as a law and rule of orthodoxy. If custom is to be taken in proof of what is right, then it is certainly competent for me to put forward on my side the custom which obtains here. If they reject this, we are clearly not bound to follow them. Therefore let God-inspired Scripture decide between us; and on whichever side be found doctrines in harmony with the word of God, in favor of that side will be cast the vote of truth."[3]

For Basil, when it came to conflicting traditions between the followers of Arius and the defenders of sound doctrine, the solution was to look to the Word of God. Scripture is the umpire over tradition, because it trumps tradition. Only what accords with the Word of God can be considered true.

Other examples could be given but the point is this: the true church submits to the Word of God as its final authority, even over religious tradition.

❖ **For Discussion:** Can you think of an example of a non-biblical religious tradition? If you were to evaluate that traditional belief or practice from a biblical perspective, what would you say about it?

## B. The Sufficiency of the Work of God

When we speak of the work of God in this lesson, we are focusing specifically on the work of salvation.

False teachers and errant movements are marked by a wrong understanding of the gospel. They attempt to add some form of human effort to that which Scripture teaches is entirely a work of God.

The biblical gospel asserts that sinners are justified before God on the basis of
_____His grace alone_____ (Luke 18:14). Salvation is the gift of God received through faith, apart from our works, based solely on the finished work of Christ.

In response to those who tried to add self-righteous works to the gospel of grace, the apostle Paul issued this stern rebuke:

> **Galatians 1:6–8**— "I am amazed that you are so quickly deserting Him who called you by the grace of Christ, for a different gospel; which is really not another; only there are some who are disturbing you and want to distort the gospel of Christ. But even if we, or an angel from heaven, should preach to you a gospel contrary to what we have preached to you, he is to be accursed!"

In Acts 16:30–31, when the Philippian jailer asked, "What must I do to be saved?" Paul's response was simple: "Believe in the Lord Jesus Christ, and you shall be saved."

In his letter to the Romans, Paul reiterated the idea that "a man is justified by faith apart from the works of the law" (Rom. 3:28). In chapter 4, he presented Abraham as an example of being justified by faith. And in chapter 5, he reiterated that because we have "been justified by faith, we have peace with God through our Lord Jesus Christ" (Rom. 5:1).

Consider some of Paul's other statements about God's grace in salvation:

> **Romans 11:6**— "If it is by grace, it is no longer on the basis of works, otherwise grace is no longer grace."

> **Ephesians 2:8–9**—"For by grace you have been saved through faith; and that not of yourselves, it is the gift of God; not as a result of works, so that no one may boast."

> **Philippians 3:8–9**—". . . not having a righteousness of my own derived from the Law, but that which is through faith in Christ, the righteousness which comes from God on the basis of faith."

> **Titus 3:4–7**—"But when the kindness of God our Savior and His love for mankind appeared, He saved us, not on the basis of deeds which we have done in righteousness, but according to His mercy, by the washing of regeneration and renewing by the Holy Spirit, whom He poured out upon us richly through Jesus Christ our Savior, so that being justified by His grace we would be made heirs according to the hope of eternal life."

Throughout his ministry, Paul emphasized the truth of the gospel, because he recognized the vital importance of what was at stake (Gal. 2:5).

❖ **For Discussion:** Given the importance of the gospel, how would you explain it to someone? What verses would you include in presenting the good news that sinners can be saved through faith in Christ?

### C. The Sanctity of the Worship of God

The true church worships the triune God (Father, Son, and Holy Spirit) in both purity of ___devotion___ and purity of _____doctrine._____

Conversely, false teachers either distort the truth about God or introduce competitors to the pure worship that He alone deserves.

As Jesus told the woman at the well:

> **John 4:23**—"An hour is coming, and now is, when the true worshipers will worship the Father in spirit and truth; for such people the Father seeks to be His worshipers."

In this verse, we see that the worship God requires is pure both in spirit (devotion) and truth (doctrine). Let's consider these two facets of acceptable worship in more detail.

**1. Purity of Devotion:** Undefiled worship is reserved for God alone. It removes _____distractions_____ and rejects _____competitors._____

The Old Testament is replete with mandates regarding the exclusive and undistracted worship that God is rightly due.

- According to Isaiah 42:8, the Lord God is a jealous God who does not share His glory with any other.

- The second of the Ten Commandments condemns those who worship idols, including those who would create a graven image for the purpose of worship (Ex. 20:4).

- One interesting Old Testament account involves the reforms made by King Hezekiah:

  > **2 Kings 18:4**— "He removed the high places and broke down the sacred pillars and cut down the Asherah. He also broke in pieces the bronze serpent that Moses had made, for until those days the sons of Israel burned incense to it; and it was called Nehushtan."

- The bronze serpent that God commanded Moses to make for the Israelites in Numbers 21:8–9 had become an object of veneration for them by the time we come to Hezekiah's day. It was competing with and contaminating the pure worship of God. As a result, Hezekiah destroyed it.

In the New Testament, all forms of idolatry are similarly condemned.

- Paul told the Corinthians to "flee from idolatry" in 1 Corinthians 10:14, while commending the Thessalonians because they "turned to God from idols to serve a living and true God" (1 Thess. 1:9).

- The apostle John similarly warned his readers in **1 John 5:21**—"Little children, guard yourselves from idols."

As these passages demonstrate, the worship God requires is a worship that is pure. True worship loves Him with all our heart, mind, soul, and strength. Thus, it is not distracted or diminished by any hint of idolatry.

**2. Purity of Doctrine:** Undefiled worship requires an accurate view of _____who God is._____

To reject or distort the truth about who God is, as He has revealed Himself in His Word, is to worship the wrong god.

Various heretical groups deny the deity of Christ, reject the truth of the Trinity, or teach that there are many gods. The worship offered by these groups is false worship because their understanding of God is erroneous.

Numerous places in Scripture make this point. We will focus on the writings of the apostle John, with specific reference to the Lord Jesus Christ.

- In his first epistle, John states that those who deny that Jesus is the Messiah are false teachers.

    **1 John 2:22**—"Who is the liar but the one who denies that Jesus is the Christ? This is the antichrist, the one who denies the Father and the Son."

- Later, he adds that those who deny the humanity of Christ are also false teachers. This was in response to an ancient heresy called *Docetism*, which taught that Jesus' human body was just an illusion. Docetism denied the reality of the incarnation, death, and resurrection of Jesus.

    Against that error, John writes:

    **1 John 4:2–3**—"By this you know the Spirit of God: every spirit that confesses that Jesus Christ has come in the flesh is from God; and every spirit that does not confess Jesus is not from God; this is the spirit of the antichrist, of which you have heard that it is coming, and now it is already in the world."

- John adds that the true church is the one that embraces the Lord Jesus as God the Son:

    **1 John 5:20**—"And we know that the Son of God has come, and has given us understanding so that we may know Him who is true; and we are in Him who is true, in His Son Jesus Christ. This is the true God and eternal life."

These same themes are repeated in other places throughout John's writings: the truth that Jesus is the Messiah, the truth that He became fully human in His incarnation, and the truth that He is God the Son.

In fact, we see all three noted in the first chapter of John's gospel:

**John 1:1**—**Jesus' Deity**—"In the beginning was the Word, and the Word was with God, and the Word was God."

**John 1:14**—**Jesus' Humanity**—"And the Word became flesh, and dwelt among us, and we saw His glory, glory as of the only begotten from the Father, full of grace and truth."

**John 1:17**—**Jesus' Messiahship**—"For the Law was given through Moses; grace and truth were realized through Jesus Christ [the Messiah]."

To deny the deity, humanity, or messiahship of the Lord Jesus constitutes a serious error, which is why John so strongly condemned the false teachers who distorted the truth about Christ (2 John 7–11).

The principle is clear: those who worship God the Son must worship Him in truth. And we can extend that principle out to the other Members of the Trinity. Those who worship the triune God must worship Him as He truly is.

❖ **For Discussion:** Review John 4:23. What can you do to make sure your worship is characterized by both purity of devotion ("spirit") and purity of doctrine ("truth")? What are some potential obstacles to that kind of God-honoring worship?

## III. APPLYING THESE PRINCIPLES TO CHURCH HISTORY

As we've seen in this lesson, the true church is like a building—established on the foundation of Jesus Christ—and defined by its commitment to several core doctrinal pillars:

1. **The Supremacy of the Word of God:** Scripture alone is our authority.

2. **The Sufficiency of the Work of God:** We are saved by grace alone through faith apart from works, based solely on the finished work of Christ.

3. **The Sanctity of the Worship of God:** We are called to worship God in purity of devotion and purity of doctrine.

If we extend the building metaphor to the whole of church history, we might picture the centuries after the apostolic age as the superstructure of the church—which rests on the foundation of Christ and continues to be defined by the pillars of biblical orthodoxy.

The doctrinal pillars discussed in this lesson provide a helpful grid for evaluating church history through a biblical lens. We will reference them again in future lessons.

The chart on the next page provides an illustration of this idea. For some people, learning church history with a chart like this is easier than an extended timeline.

❖ **For Discussion:** How can Christians today practically apply the three doctrinal pillars highlighted in this lesson? What can you do to put the authority of Scripture, the accuracy of the gospel, and the authenticity of worship into practice in your life?

# AN OVERVIEW OF CHURCH HISTORY

Over time, these pillars of biblical orthodoxy are corrupted by the elevation of man-made traditions and philosophies.

**Pillar: The WORD of God**
- Emphasis on Tradition
- *Sola Scriptura*
- Age of Reason

**Pillar: The WORK of God**
- Sacramental Works
- *Sola Fide*
- *Sola Gratia*
- Age of Reason

**Pillar: The WORSHIP of God**
- Veneration of Saints
- *Solus Christus*
- *Soli Deo Gloria*
- Age of Reason

## MODERN AGE

### Reformation

**16th Century**
- Luther
- Calvin
- Knox
- Anabaptists

**17th Century**
- Puritanism
- New England

**18th Century**
- Edwards
- Whitefield
- Great Awakening

**19th Century**
- Carey
- Judson
- Spurgeon

**20th Century**
- Modernists vs. Fundamentalists
- Evangelicals

*Modern Era*

## MIDDLE AGES

### High Middle Ages

**11th Century**
- East/West Schism
- 1st Crusade

**12th Century**
- Anselm
- Bernard
- 2nd & 3rd Crusades

**13th Century**
- 4th Crusade
- Thomas Aquinas
- Peter Waldo

**14th Century**
- Papal Schism
- John Wycliffe

**15th Century**
- Jan Hus
- Council of Constance
- Humanism

*Pre-Reformers*

### Early Middle Ages

**6th Century**
- 2nd Council of Constantinople

**7th Century**
- Rise of Islam
- 3rd Council of Constantinople

**8th Century**
- 2nd Council of Nicaea
- *Donation of Constantine*

**9th Century**
- Charlemagne
- Holy Roman Empire

**10th Century**
- Papal Corruption
- Russia Christianized

*Rise of Feudalism*

## PATRISTIC AGE

### Ante-Nicene Fathers

**1st Century**
- Pentecost
- Apostles
- Clement of Rome

**2nd Century**
- Ignatius
- Polycarp
- Justin
- Irenaeus

**3rd Century**
- Tertullian
- Origen
- Cyprian

**4th Century**
- Nicaea
- Athanasius
- 1st Council of Constantinople

**5th Century**
- Chrysostom
- Augustine
- Chalcedon

*Post-Nicene Fathers*

---

## The Foundation: The Lord Jesus Christ and the Apostolic Witness to Him
(1 Cor. 3:11; Eph. 2:20; 1 Peter 2:4–6; see also Matt. 16:16–18)

# FROM PENTECOST TO PATMOS

#### Peter, Paul, and the First-Century Church

**KEY PASSAGE: Acts 1:8**

*Jesus told His apostles, "But you will receive power when the Holy Spirit has come upon you; and you shall be My witnesses both in Jerusalem, and in all Judea and Samaria, and even to the remotest part of the earth."*

| 30 Day of Pentecost | 49 Jerusalem Council | | 64–68 Nero's Persecution | John ministers in Ephesus |
|---|---|---|---|---|
| c. 32 Conversion of Saul | Paul's Missionary Journeys | Paul in Rome | 70 Temple Destroyed | c. 95 John on Patmos |

## I. ACTS AND THE APOSTOLIC AGE

The book of Acts was written by _____Luke._____ It is a sequel to his gospel, and begins shortly after the resurrection of the Lord Jesus. The word "acts" refers to the *acts* or *deeds* of the apostles. The book of Acts focuses on the work of God accomplished through the apostles during the first few decades of the early church.

Acts covers approximately _____thirty_____ years of the history of the early church from about _____AD 30–62._____ It is the first book of church history ever written. Though unlike any other church history book, Acts was inspired by the Holy Spirit.

In Acts 1:8, just before He ascended to heaven, Jesus instructed His disciples to be His witnesses from Jerusalem and Judea to Samaria and to the ends of the world. Those geographic locations serve as an outline of the book of Acts. In Acts 1–7, the gospel of Jesus Christ is preached in Jerusalem and Judea. In Acts 8, the good news comes to Samaria. Then, starting with the conversions of Paul in Acts 9 and Cornelius in Acts 10, the gospel is taken throughout the Gentile world.

When we read about Jesus' disciples in the four gospels, they often lack faith and courage. In the book of Acts, they have undergone a radical change. Peter and his fellow apostles boldly proclaim the good news of salvation through faith in Jesus Christ. They are willing to do so, even when it results in persecution and suffering.

The radical transformation of the disciples is the result of two history-defining events:

1. _____the resurrection of Jesus Christ,_____ and

2. _____the coming of the Holy Spirit._____ As eyewitnesses to the resurrected Christ, the apostles boldly testified to the truth about Him, doing so through the Spirit's power.

Because the disciples had been sent by Jesus as His witnesses, they are known as "apostles," meaning _____"sent ones"_____ or _____"ambassadors."_____ The "Apostles of Jesus Christ" were a select group of Jesus' disciples, limited to those who had been physical eyewitnesses to the resurrected Christ, and who were directly appointed by Him. Paul says he was the last person to see the resurrected Christ (1 Cor. 15:8), meaning that no one after Paul could meet the criteria necessary to be an apostle.

Jesus gave His apostles unique authority in the church. Through the Holy Spirit, He revealed divine truth to them for the church (John 14:26–27; 16:12–14). This revelation is recorded for us in their writings, which comprise the New Testament. Each New Testament book is either written directly by an apostle (like Matthew, John, or Paul), or by someone writing under an apostle's authority (like Mark, Luke, or Jude).

To authenticate their message, God also gave the apostles the ability to _____perform miracles_____ (Acts 2:43; 5:12; 2 Cor. 12:12). These supernatural "signs" demonstrated that they were God's messengers and their testimony about Jesus Christ was true.

The apostolic period comprises a foundational age in church history (Eph. 2:20). When John, the last surviving apostle, died around the year _____100,_____ the apostolic age came to a close.

The apostolic age was a unique and unrepeated period in church history. The church leaders who lived in the following centuries did not consider themselves to be apostles. Instead, they viewed the apostles and their writings as authoritative and foundational, occupying a distinguished place in the establishment of the church.

*Recommended Reading:* To fully appreciate the content in this lesson, please read through the book of Acts. As you do, take note of the power of the gospel, as it transforms hearts and lives through the power of the Spirit.

## II. THE CHURCH IS BORN (ACTS 2)

In Matthew 16:18, Jesus promised He would build His church. That promise began to be fulfilled on the Day of _____Pentecost_____ in the year AD _____30._____ Acts 2 records what happened on that dramatic day.

About _____120_____ followers of Jesus, including the apostles, were gathered in an upper room in Jerusalem when the Holy Spirit came to indwell and empower them. The coming of the Spirit was marked by the appearance of fire and the loud sound of a rushing wind (Acts 2:1–4). Similar phenomena mark God's presence in the Old Testament (Ex. 19:16–18; 1 Kings 19:11–12).

Pentecost was one of the major feast days celebrated by the Jewish people (Deut. 16:9–10). For that reason, many Jewish pilgrims had traveled to Jerusalem from throughout the Roman Empire. These pilgrims lived in other parts of the Roman empire and, therefore, spoke native languages other than _____Aramaic_____ or _____Greek_____ (the primary languages spoken in Jerusalem).

In Acts 2, the Holy Spirit gave the apostles (and possibly others with them) the miraculous ability to speak in foreign languages they had never learned. Leaving the upper room, they went throughout Jerusalem preaching the gospel in these foreign dialects. When pilgrims to Jerusalem heard the apostles speaking fluently in their native tongues, they were amazed.

This miraculous gift is known as the gift of _____tongues._____ The Holy Spirit used it on the Day of Pentecost not only to draw a crowd, but also to demonstrate that the gospel of Jesus Christ extends to all nations.

Addressing the crowd that had gathered to witness this miracle, the apostle Peter preached a powerful gospel sermon (Acts 2:14–36). In response, some _____3,000_____ people believed. They professed faith in Christ and were_____baptized_____ as a symbolic demonstration of their repentance. On this incredible day, the church was born.

❖ **For Discussion:** Read the list of language groups that were represented on the Day of Pentecost in Acts 2:5–12. What did the gift of tongues on the Day of Pentecost illustrate about the extent of the gospel? How does this correspond to the Great Commission in Matthew 28:18–20?

## III. THE MARTYRDOM OF STEPHEN (ACTS 7)

Chapters 2–7 of the book of Acts describe the growth of the early church in Jerusalem and Judea. In Acts 2:42–47, Luke identifies the primary features of the first community of believers.

Chapters 3–4 highlight the bold preaching ministry of Peter, who proclaimed the gospel with undaunted courage. As noted above, it is remarkable to consider Peter's transformation after just a few months. The disciple who denied the Lord three times at Passover (Luke 22:54–62) faces the Jewish leaders after Pentecost with unwavering boldness (Acts 4:8–12).

Acts 5 opens with the account of Ananias and Sapphira, a sobering illustration of how serious God is about purity in worship. The remainder of that chapter highlights the continued courage of Peter and his fellow apostles. Significantly, in Acts 5:29, Peter tells the religious leaders, "We must obey God rather than men."

In Acts 6, the needs of the growing church in Jerusalem reach the point where the apostles select seven helpers to assist the congregation. These seven men include Stephen and Philip. Though their role is slightly different, these men function in some ways like the first deacons. By taking care of important logistical tasks, these seven men freed up the apostles to focus on the ministry of the Word and prayer.

In addition to serving the needs of the church, Stephen was a bold evangelist. His preaching led to his arrest by the religious leaders. In Acts 7, he delivered a powerful sermon while standing trial. Outraged by Stephen's message, the leaders responded by dragging him outside the city and stoning him to death. Those who killed Stephen laid their coats at the feet of a young man named Saul (Acts 7:58).

Stephen was the first Christian martyr. The word *martyr* comes from a Greek word meaning
_____"witness."_____ Martyrs are witnesses to Jesus Christ even to the point of death.

As a result of Stephen's martyrdom, Christians began to scatter from Jerusalem. As they did, they took the gospel with them to places like Samaria (Acts 8:1–5) and other regions throughout the Roman Empire (Acts 11:19–20). In this way, God used the death of Stephen and the resulting persecution to scatter believers throughout the Roman world, thereby beginning to fulfill the Great Commission (Matt. 28:18–20).

> ❖ **For Discussion:** In the four gospels, the disciples often exhibit faith that is frail and faltering. But in the book of Acts, they demonstrate unwavering boldness and resolve. How can we explain the dramatic difference? Practically speaking, how should we emulate their conviction and courage in our lives?

## IV. THE CONVERSIONS OF SAUL AND CORNELIUS (ACTS 9–10)

One of the primary persecutors of the church was a man named _____Saul._____ "Saul" was his _____Hebrew_____ name. Later, he would be known by his _____Greek_____ name, "Paul."

Saul was instrumental in scattering the church by persecuting Christians. Yet the Lord would later use Saul to minister to the scattered church. In fact, some of the believers who fled Jerusalem as a result of Stephen's martyrdom would be part of the church in Syrian Antioch—a church that Saul would eventually co-pastor with _____Barnabas_____ (Acts 11:19–26).

The account of Saul's conversion is well known (Acts 9:1–19; 22:3–18; 26:9–18). His encounter with Christ on the road to Damascus changed not only his life forever, but also the course of church history. The last of the apostles, he would help establish numerous churches and write more than half of the New Testament.

In God's perfect plan, a former Pharisee (Phil. 3:4–6) became the apostle to the Gentiles (Acts 26:17).

In Acts 10, Luke highlights the first Gentile conversion—the conversion of Cornelius and his family.

For 1,500 years, from the time of Moses, God worked primarily through the nation of Israel to accomplish His saving purposes. But in the church age, the gospel would extend to all people of every nation.

To underscore this, God sent Peter to preach to a Gentile man named Cornelius. The Lord prepared Peter by showing him a vision of _____unclean animals_____ (see Lev. 11) and telling him not to regard as unclean what God had cleansed (Acts 10:9–16).

Normally, the Jewish people would not enter the home of a Gentile, since doing so rendered a person ceremonially unclean. But Peter understood the point of the vision he had received. He entered the house of Cornelius and presented the gospel.

Incredibly, Cornelius and the members of his household responded to the gospel in saving faith. The Holy Spirit verified the authenticity of their faith by indwelling them in the same way He indwelt the apostles on the day of Pentecost (Acts 10:44–47).

Because they had believed in Christ and received the Holy Spirit, Peter instructed them to be baptized (Acts 10:48).

As a result of this dramatic conversion, the leaders of the church in Jerusalem recognized that the message of salvation was equally available to both Jews and Gentiles alike (Acts 11:15–18). The rest of the book of Acts highlights the gospel being taken to both Jewish and Gentile people throughout the Roman Empire.

> ❖ **For Discussion:** What was so significant about the gospel extending beyond the nation of Israel to include people from other ethnic backgrounds? Read Revelation 5:9–10. How does the composition of heaven reflect the inclusion of Gentiles into the church?

## V. THE FIRST CHURCH COUNCIL (ACTS 15)

The second half of Acts 11 records the beginning of a Jew-Gentile church in Antioch of Syria. Because of the conversion of Cornelius, the leaders of the Jerusalem church were eager to send help when they heard about the believers in Antioch.

To meet the pastoral need in Antioch, the Jerusalem church sent Barnabas (Acts 11:22). The ministry went so well that Barnabas invited Saul to come help him (v. 26).

After strengthening that church, and after a trip to Jerusalem to minister to believers there, Saul and Barnabas were sent out by the Holy Spirit (Acts 13:1–3) to go to other cities within the Roman Empire, to preach the gospel and establish churches.

Chapters 13–14 overview the trip Saul and Barnabas took, to the churches of southern Galatia. This trip is known as Paul's First Missionary Journey. In Acts 13:9, Luke begins to refer to Saul by his Greek name, Paul. This change is likely due to the fact that Paul's missionary career, beginning in Acts 13, focused primarily on the Gentiles.

In **Acts 13:38–39**, after a lengthy gospel presentation, Paul told an audience in a synagogue, "Therefore let it be known to you, brethren, that through this Man [Jesus Christ] is preached to you the forgiveness of sins; and by Him everyone who believes is justified from all things from which you could not be justified by the law of Moses" (NKJV).

These verses summarize the heart of Paul's gospel invitation—namely, that through faith in Christ, sinners can be _____forgiven_____ (from their debt of sin) and _____justified_____ (declared righteous by God). Faith in Christ accomplishes what adherence to the Law of Moses cannot provide. Salvation is by _____faith alone,_____ apart from the Law.

When Paul and Barnabas returned to Antioch after completing their missionary journey, some false teachers arrived, insisting that sinners must be circumcised and obey the Law of Moses to be saved.

This resulted in a conflict about the essence of the gospel (Acts 15:1–5; Gal. 2:4–5). Are sinners saved by faith in Christ alone, as Paul had been preaching? Or do they also need to follow the Law of Moses?

To settle the conflict, Paul and Barnabas travelled to Jerusalem to meet with the apostles and church elders there. Paul met with some of the leaders privately (according to Gal. 2:1–10), before a public council meeting took place (Acts 15:6).

At the council, which took place around AD 49 or 50, Peter defended the true gospel with these words:

> **Acts 15:7–11**—"Brethren, you know that in the early days God made a choice among you, that by my mouth the Gentiles would hear the word of the gospel and believe. And God, who knows the heart, testified to them giving them the Holy Spirit, just as He also did to us; and He made no distinction between us and them, cleansing their hearts by faith. Now therefore why do you put God to the test by placing upon the neck of the disciples a yoke which neither our fathers nor we have been able to bear? But we believe that we are saved through the grace of the Lord Jesus, in the same way as they also are."

As Peter explained, sinners are saved "through the grace of the Lord Jesus" because their hearts are cleansed "by faith." In this way, Peter affirmed the truth of the gospel that Paul had proclaimed on his missionary journey (in Acts 13).

Under the leadership of _____James,_____ the brother of Jesus, the council affirmed the ministry of Paul and Barnabas. Gentile believers were not required to follow the Law of Moses, though they were instructed to avoid immorality and to be sensitive to the consciences of fellow believers from a Jewish background.

Later, Paul learned that the churches he and Barnabas had planted on their first missionary journey (in southern Galatia) were being threatened by these same false teachers. He responded by writing a letter to express his concern. That letter is the Epistle to the Galatians.

❖ **For Discussion:** What were the key differences between the gospel Paul preached and the errant gospel of the false teachers? Read Galatians 1:6–9. Why is it so important to understand the gospel correctly?

## VI. ADDITIONAL MISSIONARY JOURNEYS (ACTS 16–28)

Most English Bibles have maps located in the back. If you've ever looked at them, you've likely seen a map of Paul's missionary journeys.

Paul's second missionary journey started as a return trip to the churches he and Barnabas had planted on their earlier trip. This time Paul traveled with _____Silas_____ (Acts 15:40) and _____Timothy_____ (Acts 16:1–3).

The scope of their trip was expanded by the Holy Spirit who, in Acts 16:9–10, gave Paul a vision of a man from Macedonia asking for help. Paul and his companions responded by traveling to cities in Macedonia and Greece, like Philippi, Thessalonica, Berea, Athens, Corinth, and Ephesus.

In each city, Paul preached the gospel faithfully. He began in the _____synagogue,_____ reasoning with his Jewish hearers from ____the Old Testament.____ When he was no longer welcome there, he would preach to the _____Gentiles_____ of that city.

During his second missionary journey, Paul wrote 1 and 2 Thessalonians.

Paul's third missionary journey begins in Acts 18:23. Again, he travelled to cities where he had already been, like Ephesus and Corinth, to strengthen the churches there. During his time in Ephesus, Paul trained the disciples for more than two years (Acts 19:8–10). As a result, churches throughout _____Asia Minor_____ were planted in places like Colossae.

Despite the dangers Paul faced (2 Cor. 11:23–29), his commitment to the Lord never wavered. He boldly proclaimed the good news of salvation through Christ.

Paul's third missionary journey ended in Jerusalem (Acts 21:17). During this journey, Paul wrote 1 and 2 Corinthians and Romans.

In Jerusalem, Paul was seized by an angry mob in the Temple, who mistakenly thought he had invited Gentiles into the Temple grounds (Acts 21:28). Paul was rescued by Roman soldiers, who took him into custody.

Paul spent the next two years imprisoned in Caesarea, on the Mediterranean coast. Luke, who was one of Paul's traveling companions, likely wrote his gospel during this time.

After appearing before King Herod Agrippa II, Paul was deemed innocent. However, because he had appealed to Caesar (Acts 26:32), he was sent to Rome to stand trial.

In Acts 27, Paul found himself on a transport ship bound for Rome. During the voyage, Paul and his fellow shipmates survived a dramatic shipwreck.

Eventually making it to Rome, Paul was placed under house arrest for approximately _____two years_____ (Acts 28:30–31). This "first Roman imprisonment" occurred from about AD 60–62. Luke likely wrote the book of Acts during this time, since the narrative of Acts ends at this point.

While under house arrest, Paul penned what are known as his "prison epistles"—Ephesians, Colossians, Philemon, and Philippians.

❖ **For Discussion:** Read 2 Corinthians 11:23–29. Paul wrote this during his second missionary journey. What stands out to you about the sacrifices he was willing to make for the sake of Christ?

## VII. AFTER THE BOOK OF ACTS

With the closing chapter of Acts, the Spirit-inspired record of church history ends.

Nonetheless, with indirect evidence from certain biblical passages and historical information from other sources, we can piece together a general sense of what happened in the final few decades of first-century church history.

The evidence suggests Paul was released from house arrest. He apparently traveled to ___Troas and Miletus___ (2 Tim. 4:13, 20), _____Crete_____ (Titus 1:5), and even _____Spain_____ (Rom. 15:23–24). Some of the earliest church fathers confirm that Paul made it to Spain.

During this time, Paul wrote the "pastoral epistles" of 1 Timothy and Titus.

In the summer of AD 64, a massive fire broke out in the city of Rome. Much of the city was either destroyed or severely damaged.

When public opinion began to suspect Emperor Nero was behind the fire, he shifted the blame to the Christians and began to persecute them in horrific ways. The ancient Roman historian Tacitus provides a record of these events, noting that believers were sometimes lit on fire like human torches, or sewn in animal skins and fed to wild beasts.

During this persecution, the apostle Peter (who had come to Rome earlier to minister there) was arrested and executed by being crucified upside down. Prior to his death, Peter wrote two epistles from Rome to churches in Asia Minor, warning them about coming persecution and the threat of false teachers.

Paul was also arrested and imprisoned in a Roman dungeon. This second imprisonment provides the context for his second letter to Timothy. Shortly after penning that epistle, Paul was beheaded as a martyr for Christ.

Nero's persecution also provides the historical backdrop for the book of Hebrews—in which the author warns his readers not to return to Judaism, thereby defecting from Christ, merely to avoid persecution. Throughout church history, most commentators believed Paul to be the author of Hebrews. If it was not Paul, it was undoubtedly one of his close associates (like Luke or Apollos).

Nero's persecution ended with his death in AD 68.

Around that time, a revolt began in Judea that resulted in Jerusalem being attacked and the Temple destroyed (in AD 70) by the army of Emperor Vespasian.

According to tradition, the Christians in Jerusalem fled the city prior to the arrival of the Roman army. They found refuge in Pella, a town within the jurisdiction of King Herod Agrippa II. Interestingly, this was the same king before whom Paul gave a defense in Acts 26. Herod may have remembered Paul (see Acts 26:27) and was therefore inclined to grant asylum to these believers.

The 80s and 90s feature the ministry of the apostle _____John._____ At some point, he moved from Jerusalem to Ephesus, ministering in the region of Asia Minor.

John likely wrote his gospel and three epistles in the 80s.

His exile to Patmos probably occurred in the mid-90s, during the reign of Emperor Domitian. It was during his exile that he received a final revelation from the Lord Jesus. Because John was the last surviving apostle, the book of Revelation is also the last book of the New Testament canon.

❖ **For Discussion:** In chapters 2–3, the book of Revelation addresses seven churches from the region of Asia Minor. Some of these churches were faithful. Some had compromised. What would you identify as the primary marks of a faithful church?

## VIII. COMING FULL CIRCLE

A survey of the apostolic age of church history teaches many important lessons. Here are three to consider:

1. The good news of salvation is intended for all people of every ethnic background and language group. Sinners can be forgiven and justified though faith in Christ, apart from the works of the Law. The offer of the gospel is possible because of the life, death, and resurrection of Jesus Christ.

2. Followers of the Lord Jesus are called to be His witnesses, speaking with conviction and standing with courage. The apostles modeled that kind of boldness. In the face of growing hostility and even violent persecution, they stood firm for Christ no matter the cost. As Peter told the religious leaders in Acts 5, "We must obey God rather than men." That ought to be our mindset too.

3. The Lord has been faithful to fulfill His promise to build the church. To observe the gospel prevail against all odds, from the book of Acts to the present, is to see that promise unfold. The church continues to grow, even in the face of severe opposition. For those who are part of Christ's church, how encouraging it is to know that we are part of a movement that cannot fail because it is guaranteed by God Himself.

❖ **For Discussion:** What other lessons stand out to you from your study of first-century church history?

# PART II

# THE PATRISTIC PERIOD*

## 2ND–5TH CENTURIES

\* The term *patristic* comes from a Latin word meaning
"father." The "Patristic Period" refers to the era of the
early church fathers—that is, early Christian
leaders after the time of the apostles.

**KEY PASSAGE: 2 Timothy 2:2**

*"The things which you have heard from me in the presence of many witnesses, entrust these to faithful men who will be able to teach others also."*

~100
**Martyrdom of Clement**

~117
**Martyrdom of Ignatius**

155
**Martyrdom of Polycarp**

~95
**Clement, First Epistle**

*The Didache*

*Epistle to Diognetus*

## I. IN THE FOOTSTEPS OF THE APOSTLES

In contemporary churches, 2 Timothy 2:2 is often viewed as a model for multigenerational ministry. That is certainly a valid way to think about that verse. But when Paul first wrote about "faithful men" and "others also," he undoubtedly had specific people in mind.

When we look back at early church history, we discover the names of some of those faithful men. They were part of the generation of believers who came immediately after the apostles.

As noted in Lesson 2, they did not view themselves as apostles, but rather as pastors and elders who had been entrusted with the truth. Their charge was to guard the treasure they had received and faithfully preserve it for future generations.

We refer to these early Christian leaders as the "Apostolic Fathers." The term "church fathers" should be thought of in the sense of "founding fathers." They were the early leaders of the church. In this case, their close connection to the apostles makes them "Apostolic Fathers."

The "Apostolic Fathers" include the authors of a number of works that have survived to the present. In this lesson, we will consider five of these early authors:

1. Clement of Rome

2. Ignatius of Antioch

3. Polycarp of Smyrna

4. The author of *The Didache*

5. The author of *The Letter to Diognetus*

English translations of the writings of these early Christian leaders are freely available online. They can be accessed with a quick web search.

❖ **For Discussion:** How many generations of Christian leadership are represented in 2 Timothy 2:2? What should that principle of multi-generational leadership look like in the church today?

## II. CLEMENT OF ROME (DIED C. 100)

Clement pastored the church in _____Rome_____ from around _____90–100._____ To put that in perspective, he was pastoring the Roman congregation when the apostle John was exiled to the island of Patmos.

Some have noted the possibility that the Clement mentioned in Philippians 4:3 is this same person. Though possible (since the epistle of Philippians was written in the early 60s), that connection cannot be confirmed with certainty.

Clement wrote one letter that has survived. It was likely written in the mid-90s, addressed to the church in Corinth from the church in Rome. Consequently, it is known as Clement's *Epistle to the Corinthians*. Sometimes it is called *1 Clement*. This is due to the fact that another early Christian work, called *2 Clement*, was historically associated with Clement of Rome. However, modern scholarship has shown that Clement was probably not the author of *2 Clement*.

The primary issue addressed in Clement's letter is division within the Corinthian congregation. Forty years after the apostle Paul addressed the same issue (in 1 Cor. 1), Clement articulates his concerns about the infighting and disunity that had once again crept into the Corinthian congregation.

Clement's letter demonstrates that he was familiar with the writings of Paul, including Paul's epistle to the Romans.

In one important passage, Clement explains that believers are justified by faith apart from works, just like Abraham was. He writes this:

> **Clement of Rome:** "And so we, having been called through His will in Christ Jesus, are not justified through ourselves or through our own wisdom or understanding or piety or works that we have done in holiness of heart, but through faith, by which the Almighty God has justified all who have existed from the beginning; to whom be the glory forever and ever. Amen."[1]

Clement rightly understood that justification is a gift of God's grace, received by faith apart from works. It is not obtained through self-effort ("ourselves"), human ingenuity or cleverness ("our own wisdom or understanding"), works righteousness ("works which we have wrought"), or personal piety ("in holiness of heart"). In this way, Clement affirms the gospel of grace from the earliest period of post-apostolic church history.

❖ **For Discussion:** Based on the quote above, how would you describe Clement's understanding of the means of justification? Read Ephesians 2:4–9. How does Clement's statement coordinate with Paul's declaration that salvation is by grace through faith, apart from works?

## III. IGNATIUS OF ANTIOCH (DIED C. 117)

The church of Antioch was established in the 40s, under the pastoral leadership of Barnabas and Paul (Acts 11).

Though not mentioned in the book of Acts, Ignatius became the pastor there sometime in the late first-century. A fifth-century tradition suggests that _____Peter_____ gave instructions for Ignatius to be appointed the pastor of the Antiochene church.

Tradition also indicates that Ignatius, along with Polycarp (below), was a disciple of the Apostle John.

Seven of Ignatius's letters have survived. Both a shorter and longer version of these letters exists, with the shorter version likely being the original. Like Clement, Ignatius wrote these letters to churches.

One theme Ignatius highlights is that Christians gather for worship on Sunday, which is the Lord's Day. For example, in his *Epistle to the Magnesians*, he writes,

> **Ignatius:** [We are] "no longer observing the Sabbath, but living in the observance of the Lord's Day, on which also our life has sprung up again by Him and His death."[2]

The church's practice of meeting on Sunday, not Saturday, was already established in the New Testament (Acts 20:7; 1 Cor. 16:2). But it is interesting to see it reiterated by an early Christian leader like Ignatius.

In his writings, Ignatius indicates his belief that each local congregation should have only one "bishop" or lead/senior pastor, even though a church might also have multiple "elders" and "deacons." Ignatius seems to stress this point out of a concern that multiple bishops could lead to potential division and disunity within churches.[3]

In the New Testament, the roles of "bishop" and "elder" are synonymous (Acts 20:17, 28; Titus 1:5–7; 1 Peter 5:1–5). Starting with Ignatius, these roles became distinct in church history—with the role of bishop being elevated above the role of elder in terms of authority in the church.

Ignatius was martyred in _____Rome_____ around the year 117. According to tradition, he was fed to wild beasts, possibly in the Circus Maximus—an arena similar to the Colosseum.

> ❖ **For Discussion:** In teaching that Christians gather on the Lord's Day (Sunday) rather than the Sabbath, Ignatius was following the lead of the New Testament. Read Acts 20:7; 1 Corinthians 16:2; Colossians 2:16–17; Revelation 1:10. What do these passages teach about the Lord's Day? Why do Christians gather on the Lord's Day (see John 20:1, 19)?

## IV. POLYCARP OF SMYRNA (DIED C. 155)

Polycarp, whose name means "fruitful," was a disciple of the apostle _____John._____

He pastored the church in Smyrna, near Ephesus, for much of the first half of the second century. Smyrna is one of the seven churches listed in the book of Revelation (Rev. 2:8–10).

His *Epistle to the Philippians* is his only surviving letter. It was likely written around the time of the martyrdom of Ignatius. That these two pastors knew each other is evident from references in their letters.

Polycarp's letter begins with these words:

> **Polycarp:** "I also rejoice because your firmly rooted faith, renowned from the earliest times, still perseveres and bears fruit to our Lord Jesus Christ, who endured for our sins, facing even death, whom God raised up, having loosed the birth pangs of Hades. Though you have not seen Him, you believe in Him with an inexpressible and glorious joy (which many desire

to experience), knowing that by grace you have been saved, not because of works, but by the will of God through Jesus Christ."[4]

Significantly, the letter contains more than one hundred citations of or allusions to the New Testament (from 17 different New Testament books). This demonstrates that Polycarp was familiar with apostolic writings, and viewed those writings as authoritative. Polycarp was representative of the early church in this regard.

Consider some of the convictions Polycarp expresses in his letter:

▶ Jesus is both King and Judge.

> **Polycarp:** "Therefore prepare for action and serve God in fear and truth, leaving behind empty and meaningless talk and the error of the crowd, and believing in the one who raised our Lord Jesus Christ from the dead and gave Him glory and a throne at His right hand. To Him all things in heaven and on earth were subjected, whom every breathing creature serves, who is coming as judge of the living and the dead, for whose blood God will hold responsible those who disobey."[5]

▶ We must submit to God and His Word.

> **Polycarp:** "So then, let us serve Him with fear and all reverence, just as He Himself has commanded, as did the apostles who preached the gospel to us, and the prophets who announced in advance the coming of our Lord."[6]

▶ The believer's hope in Jesus Christ is greater than persecution.

> **Polycarp:** "Let us, therefore, hold steadfastly and unceasingly to our hope and the guarantee of our righteousness, who is Christ Jesus, who bore our sins in His own body upon the tree, who committed no sin, and no deceit was found in His mouth; instead, for our sakes He endured all things, in order that we might live in Him. Let us, therefore, become imitators of His patient endurance, and if we should suffer for the sake of His name, let us glorify Him."[7]

▶ Because our hope is sure, we are able to stand firm in the faith and focus on loving others.

> **Polycarp:** "Stand fast, therefore, in these things and follow the example of the Lord, firm and immovable in faith, loving the family of believers, cherishing one another, united in the truth, giving way to one another in the gentleness of the Lord, despising no one."[8]

The clarity of these convictions in Polycarp's letter should encourage our hearts. Polycarp's perspective was grounded in the teaching of God's Word. That explains why these truths resonate with our hearts today.

The courageous convictions that characterized Polycarp are perhaps most clearly seen in his martyrdom.

The account of his death is recorded in *The Martyrdom of Polycarp*, which is one of the earliest accounts of Christian martyrdom ever written.

By the time Polycarp was arrested for being a Christian, he had been a pastor in Smyrna for a long time. When the soldiers came to arrest him, he offered to serve them dinner. They accepted. While they were eating, Polycarp devoted himself to prayer.

When he was brought before the Roman governor for his trial, the governor urged him to deny Christ and thereby preserve his life. Polycarp famously replied, "Eighty and six years have I served Him, and He never did me any injury. How then could I blaspheme my King and my Savior?"[9]

When it became clear that Polycarp would not recant, he was sentenced to be burned at the stake. Even in the face of suffering and death, Polycarp's faith never wavered.

In recounting the faithfulness of this second-century pastor, *The Martyrdom of Polycarp* concludes with these words:

> **Martyrdom of Polycarp**: "This, then, is the account of the blessed Polycarp, who, being the twelfth that was martyred in Smyrna (reckoning those also of Philadelphia), yet occupies a place of his own in the memory of all men, insomuch that he is everywhere spoken of by the heathen themselves. He was not merely an illustrious teacher, but also a pre-eminent martyr, whose martyrdom all desire to imitate, as having been altogether consistent with the Gospel of Christ. For, having through patience overcome the unjust governor, and thus acquired the crown of immortality, he now, with the apostles and all the righteous [in heaven], rejoicingly glorifies God, even the Father, and blesses our Lord Jesus Christ, the Savior of our souls, the Governor of our bodies, and the Shepherd of the Universal Church throughout the world."[10]

Like Clement, Ignatius, and the other early martyrs, Polycarp died as a witness to the truth of the gospel of Jesus Christ.

Armed with biblical convictions, Polycarp lived out the implications of his faith even to the end.

❖ **For Discussion:** What convictions propelled Polycarp to be faithful to Christ even to the point of death? What practical steps can Christians take to develop those same convictions in their hearts and lives?

## V. *THE DIDACHE* (LATE-FIRST OR EARLY-SECOND CENTURY)

*The Didache* (meaning the *Teaching*) was an early manual of _____Christian ethics._____ It is also known by a more complete title, "The Teaching of the Lord through the Twelve Apostles to the Nations." Its purpose was to explain the way that believers are to live as followers of Jesus.

It was not written by an apostle or under apostolic authorization, and is therefore not part of the New Testament canon. Nonetheless, in church history, it was regarded as a summary of apostolic teaching.

*The Didache* begins with a section on the two ways—the way of life (the Christian life) and the way of death. Much of this section is drawn from the teachings of Jesus. For example:

> **The Didache**: "There are two ways, one of life and one of death, and there is a great difference between these two ways. Now this is the way of life. First, you shall love God, who made you. Second, you shall love your neighbor as yourself; but whatever you do not wish to happen to you, do not do to another."[11]

One interesting note, from a modern evangelical perspective, is *The Didache's* inclusion of abortion under the banner of murder.

> **The Didache**: "The second commandment of the teaching is: You shall not murder; you shall not commit adultery; you shall not corrupt children; you shall not be sexually immoral; you shall not steal; you shall not practice magic; you shall not engage in sorcery; you shall not abort a child or commit infanticide."[12]

In addition to ethical matters, *The Didache* also gives instructions for church practice, addressing topics such as baptism, the celebration of the Lord's Supper, fasting, and how to handle itinerant teachers.

❖ **For Discussion:** Read Matthew 7:13–14. *The Didache* emphasizes the difference between those on the narrow way and those on the broad road. If you were to describe the attitudes and actions that should characterize those on "the way that leads to life," what things would you emphasize?

## VI. *EPISTLE TO DIOGNETUS* (MID TO LATE SECOND CENTURY)

This letter was written by an anonymous author, who simply identifies himself as a "Mathetes," the Greek word for "disciple."

The letter is addressed to someone named Diognetus. Some have suggested the letter was written to a tutor of Emperor Marcus Aurelius by the same name. (Marcus Aurelius reigned as Roman Emperor from 161–180). However, that connection is uncertain.

The letter provides a beautiful presentation of the good news of salvation through Jesus Christ. Writing to a non-believer, the author explains that, in Christ, sinners can find both _____forgiveness for sin_____ and _____eternal life._____

In this extended section from the *Epistle to Diognetus*, consider the glories of the gospel:

> ***Epistle to Diognetus:*** "But when our wickedness had reached its height, and it had been clearly shown that its reward, punishment and death, was impending over us; and when the time had come which God had before appointed for manifesting His own kindness and power, how the one love of God, through exceeding regard for men, did not regard us with hatred, nor thrust us away, nor remember our iniquity against us, but showed great long-suffering, and bore with us, He Himself took on Him the burden of our iniquities, He gave His own Son as a ransom for us, the holy One for transgressors, the blameless One for the wicked, the righteous One for the unrighteous, the incorruptible One for the corruptible, the immortal One for them that are mortal. For what other thing was capable of covering our sins than His righteousness? By what other one was it possible that we, the wicked and ungodly, could be justified, than by the only Son of God? O sweet exchange! O unsearchable operation! O benefits surpassing all expectation! That the wickedness of many should be hid in a single righteous One, and that the righteousness of One should justify many transgressors!"[13]

In this way, the author contrasts the sinner's total inability with the all-sufficient sacrifice and perfect righteousness of Christ. Through faith in Him, believers are both forgiven and justified. They are pardoned for sin, because Jesus paid their penalty on the cross. And they are declared righteous by God, because they have been clothed in the spotless righteousness of their Savior.

Christians today should be encouraged to see such a clear articulation of the gospel message from the early centuries of church history.

❖ **For Discussion:** If you wrote a letter to an unbelieving friend or family member about the gospel, how would you describe the good news of salvation in Jesus Christ? Is there someone to whom you would consider sending a letter like that?

## VII. FINAL THOUGHTS

After surveying a number of the Apostolic Fathers, we can be encouraged to see that there were "faithful men" who lived after the apostles (2 Tim. 2:2). Though neither inerrant nor authoritative, their writings demonstrate an earnest commitment both to preserve and practice the teaching of the apostles. They sought to live according to the Word of God.

They also sought to preserve the truth of the gospel. In the writings of Clement and Polycarp, and also in the *Epistle to Diognetus*, we find clear articulations of the truth that salvation is by grace through faith in Christ; it is not received on the basis of works.

Finally, their faithfulness was demonstrated even to the point of death. Clement, Ignatius, and Polycarp all died as martyrs (or "witnesses") of Jesus Christ. Their courage, and the conviction that fueled it, stands as a compelling reminder for believers today to emulate their example of faithful fortitude.

❖ **For Discussion:** What stood out to you about the Apostolic Fathers? As you consider their example, what lessons did you learn that you can begin to put into practice?

# CONTENDING FOR THE FAITH

Justin, Irenaeus, and the Pre-Nicene Church

---

**KEY PASSAGE: Jude 3–4**

*"Beloved, while I was making every effort to write you about our common salvation, I felt the necessity to write to you appealing that you contend earnestly for the faith which was once for all handed down to the saints. For certain persons have crept in unnoticed, those who were long beforehand marked out for this condemnation, ungodly persons who turn the grace of our God into licentiousness and deny our only Master and Lord, Jesus Christ."*

| ~150 Justin writes his *First Apology* | Irenaeus writes *Against Heresies* | Tertullian writes from Carthage | ~240 Tertullian dies |
| --- | --- | --- | --- |

| ~165 Martyrdom of Justin | ~202 Martyrdom of Irenaeus | Origen writes and teaches from Caesarea | ~253 Origen dies |
| --- | --- | --- | --- |

---

## I. INTRODUCTION

From the very beginning, the church has faced threats from both without and within.

Externally, the church has endured opposition and persecution, from both proponents of false religion and hostile governments.

Internally, the church has been threatened by false teachers. They claim to be part of the church but promote doctrines or practices that are antithetical to genuine Christianity.

God has always raised up leaders in the church to respond on both fronts.

_____"Apologetics"_____ (from a Greek word meaning "legal defense") refers to a defense of the faith in the face of external attack. First Peter 3:14–15 is a key passage in this regard. Here Peter writes:

> **1 Peter 3:14–15**—"Do not fear their intimidation, and do not be troubled, but sanctify Christ as Lord in your hearts, always being ready to make a defense to everyone who asks you to give an account for the hope that is in you, yet with gentleness and reverence."

_____"Polemics"_____ (from a Greek word meaning "war") refers to theological disputation or debate. It speaks of contending for the truth in the face of internal attack from false teaching. A key verse in this regard is 2 Corinthians 10:5, where the apostle Paul talks about casting down the false arguments of his opponents.

> **2 Corinthians 10:5**—"We are destroying speculations and every lofty thing raised up against the knowledge of God, and we are taking every thought captive to the obedience of Christ."

In this lesson, we will consider a number of significant Christian leaders in the second and third centuries. When faced with threats from both outside and inside the church, these leaders rushed to defend the truth and refute error (Titus 1:9).

The term "Pre-Nicene" or "Ante-Nicene" refers to the time period before the Council of Nicaea in 325.

## II. THE APOLOGISTS

The Lord Jesus promised that His followers would be hated by unbelievers in the world. In **John 15:18**, He told His disciples, "If the world hates you, you know that it has hated Me before it hated you."

In **2 Timothy 3:12,** the apostle Paul gave a similar warning to Timothy: "Indeed, all who desire to live godly in Christ Jesus will be persecuted."

As we move into the second century of church history, believers continued to face persecution and hostility from the non-Christian society around them.

Christians were often viewed as troublemakers and a public nuisance. Roman society's negative attitude towards Christianity was perpetuated by a number of vicious rumors.

► _____Atheism_____—Christians were accused of being atheists because they flatly rejected the pantheon of Roman deities. When natural disasters occurred, unbelievers were quick to blame the Christians, insisting the gods were angry because the Christians were turning people away from them.

► _____Insurrection_____—Early Christians were also suspected of sedition and accused of being insurrectionists, in part because their worldview was so radically different from the society around them. For example, they refused to participate in anything that smacked of the worship of Caesar. They would not even declare, "Caesar is Lord," insisting instead that only Jesus is Lord (Rom. 10:9).

► _____Immorality_____—A third rumor suggested that Christians participated in sexual immorality at their secret meetings. The "love feast" (see Jude 12) was misconstrued by the imaginations of a pagan society, as were affectionate familial terms like "brother" and "sister."

► _____Cannibalism_____—Perhaps most shocking of all, Christians were even accused of being cannibals. This rumor was sparked by a misunderstanding of the Lord's Table. When outsiders heard the phrases, "This is My body" and "This is My blood," they failed to understand their symbolic meaning.

In response to these false rumors, a number of early Christian apologists wrote to defend the faith by setting the record straight. The most well-known of these apologists was a man named Justin Martyr (see below).

❖ **For Discussion:** How do unbelievers view Christians in our society? Is their perception accurate or inaccurate? What should believers do to make a defense in the midst of a secular culture?

## III. JUSTIN MARTYR (DIED C. 165)

Justin was born around _____100_____ into a non-Christian family. As a young man, Justin searched for truth in various philosophical systems. But he was never satisfied until he met an elderly Christian man who explained the gospel to him. From that point forward, Justin embraced Christianity as the true philosophy.

After becoming a Christian, Justin moved to Rome where he started a training school.

Justin used the concept of _____the divine Logos_____ (or _____"Word"_____ from John 1) as a way to build bridges to those steeped in Greek philosophy. The concept of the eternal Logos (or "eternal Word") was prominent in certain Greek philosophical systems.

Though some of Justin's works have been lost, his *First Apology* (or Defense), *Second Apology*, and *Dialogue with Trypho* have survived.

Justin's *First Apology* was a defense of the Christian faith, addressed to Emperor Antonius Pius along with the Roman Senate. His *Second Apology* was also addressed to the Roman Senate. These treatises might be thought of as "open letters" to the government, in which Justin explains why Christianity should not be the subject of imperial persecution.

His *Dialogue with Trypho* records his conversation with a Jewish man about whether Jesus truly is the Messiah. Justin musters numerous arguments from the Old Testament to show that Jesus is both the promised Savior and the divine Son of God.

After debating a Roman philosopher named Crescens, Justin was denounced to authorities as a Christian. He was beheaded around the year 165, during the reign of Emperor Marcus Aurelius.

In his *First Apology*, written around the year 150, Justin describes an early church service:

> **Justin**: "And on the day called Sunday, all who live in cities or in the country gather together to one place and the memoirs of the apostles or the writings of the prophets are read, as long as time permits; then, when the reader has ceased, the president [pastor] verbally instructs, and exhorts to the imitation of these good things. Then we all rise together and pray, and, as we before said, when our prayer is ended, bread and wine and water are brought, and the president in like manner offers prayers and thanksgivings, according to his ability, and the people assent, saying Amen; and there is a distribution to each, and a participation of that over which thanks have been given, and to those who are absent a portion is sent by the deacons. And they who are well to do, and willing, give what each thinks fit; and what is collected is deposited with the president, who [cares for] the orphans and widows, and those who, through sickness or any other cause, are in want, and those who are in bonds, and the strangers sojourning among us, and in a word takes care of all who are in need. But Sunday is the day on which we all hold our common assembly, because it is the first day on which God, having wrought a change in the darkness and matter, made the world; and Jesus Christ our Savior on the same day rose from the dead."[1]

Justin's description provides a good idea of what took place in a second-century church service.

Notice at least six important components of the worship service:

1. Scripture was read, from both the New Testament ("the memoirs of the apostles") and the Old Testament ("the writings of the prophets").

2. The pastor preached a message ("discourse"), exhorting the people to obey the things they had just heard from the Scripture.

3. The congregation prayed together.

4. The congregation participated in commemorating the Lord's Supper.

5. A free-will offering was collected to meet the needs of fellow saints.

6. The service took place on Sunday, the day on which Jesus rose from the dead.

Believers today can be encouraged when they participate in those same activities at their local church. Faithful churches from the second century to today have been characterized by these Bible-based practices.

❖ **For Discussion:** What encourages you most about Justin's description of a second-century church service? What did you find to be most surprising about his description?

## IV. THE POLEMICISTS

In addition to persecution, the New Testament also warns Christians about the reality of _____false teachers._____

For example, Paul exhorted the Ephesian elders with these words:

> **Acts 20:29–30**—"I know that after my departure savage wolves will come in among you, not sparing the flock; and from among your own selves men will arise, speaking perverse things, to draw away the disciples after them."

From the earliest stages of church history, we see both the rise of false teachers (who seek to distort the truth) and the resolve of genuine believers (who are zealous to defend the truth).

These ancient heresies include:

▶ _____Gnosticism_____—a diverse group of false movements that each claimed to possess the "secret knowledge" of salvation. The Greek word gnosis means "knowledge." Gnosticism was characterized by forms of dualism, in which material things were viewed as inferior or evil in comparison with spiritual realities. As a result, Gnostic groups generally denied that Jesus had a real, physical body. Instead, they wrongly claimed He only had the appearance of a body (see 2 John 7).

▶ _____Marcionism_____—in keeping with Gnostic ideas about the inferiority of the physical world, Marcion of Sinope (died c. 160) taught that the God of the Old Testament was an evil deity, because He created this physical universe. Marcion further insisted that Jesus was sent by an unknown god to save people from the God of the Old Testament. To purport his views, Marcion rejected the Old Testament and most of the writings of the apostles. In response to Marcion and other false teachers, Christians began to create lists of the books that the church recognized as canonical.

▶ _____Modalism_____—a denial of the Trinity that taught that sometimes God operates in the mode of the Father, sometimes in the mode of the Son, and sometimes in the mode of the Holy Spirit—but never as three distinct, co-eternal persons. According to this view, the Father became the Son at the incarnation, leading to the conclusion that it was the Father who suffered on the cross. This error, called Patripassianism ("Father's suffering"), was rejected as heretical by the early church. A primary proponent of Modalism was Sabellius, who taught in Rome in the early third century.

▶ _____Montanism_____—a movement known as the New Prophecy by its followers. It was started by a self-proclaimed prophet named Montanus (late second century), who was accompanied by two prophetesses, Maximillia and Priscilla. Insisting that the Holy Spirit was giving them new revelation for the church, they often prophesied in ecstatic and dramatic ways. Their prophecies promoted extreme forms of self-ascetism and predicted that Jesus would return shortly to set up the New Jerusalem in the region of Phrygia. The church ultimately rejected the movement as heretical.

In response to the errors of false teaching, the church was careful to articulate its doctrinal convictions. These theological convictions were grounded in the authority of Scripture, yet their expression was often clarified in the face of heretical attack.

We will consider a couple of the early polemicists (those who engaged and refuted false teaching) in this lesson.

## A. Irenaeus of Lyons (died 202)

Irenaeus (pronounced "ear-wren-nay-us") was born around the year _____130._____

As a young man, he heard Polycarp of Smyrna, thereby linking him to the apostolic fathers.

He became the bishop of a church in the Roman province of Gaul, in what is now Lyons, France.

His most famous work, known as _____*Against Heresies,*_____ was written to refute the false teachings of Gnosticism.

▶ Irenaeus pointed to the Scriptures to defend the truth and also to refute the errors of the Gnostics.

**Irenaeus:** "We have learned from none others the plan of our salvation, than from those through whom the Gospel has come down to us, which they did at one time proclaim in public, and, at a later period, by the will of God, handed down to us in the Scriptures, to be the ground and pillar of our faith."[2]

▶ Irenaeus also identified the basic Christian beliefs that had been handed down from the time of the apostles. Here is how he described those theological truths:

**Irenaeus:** "[The] ancient tradition of the apostles [is] believing in one God, the Creator of heaven and earth, and all things therein, by means of Christ Jesus, the Son of God; who, because of His surpassing love towards His creation, condescended to be born of the virgin, He Himself uniting man through Himself to God, and having suffered under Pontius Pilate, and rising again, and having been received up in splendor, shall come in glory, the Savior of those who are saved, and the Judge of those who are judged, and sending into eternal fire those who transform the truth, and despise His Father and His advent."[3]

▶ Believers today should be encouraged to see those core Christian doctrines articulated with clarity and defended with boldness by this second-century church leader.

Speaking of boldness, Irenaeus was martyred around the year 202 when persecution against Christianity erupted in the region of Gaul.

## B. Tertullian of Carthage (c. 155–240)

Born in North Africa, in the city of Carthage, Tertullian is traditionally thought to have been trained as a lawyer. Whether or not he received such training, he exhibits a high degree of education and rhetorical ability in his writings.

He was the first major Christian author to write predominantly in Latin rather than Greek. Consequently, he is known as the ___"Father of Latin (or Western) Theology."___

In describing the reality of God's three-in-oneness, Tertullian was the first person to use the Latin term ___"Trinity."___ Tertullian firmly upheld the truth that there is only one God. Yet, he also recognized that the Trinity consists of three Persons—Father, Son, and Holy Spirit.

As a defender of Christianity, Tertullian wrote an *Apology* (Defense) as well as a number of polemical works, including a polemic *Against Marcion*.

Tertullian was also strongly opposed to the idea that Christianity should be influenced by ___Greek philosophy.___ Identifying Greek philosophy by its birthplace (Athens), and the church by its birthplace (Jerusalem), Tertullian asked the rhetorical question:

> **Tertullian:** "What indeed has Athens to do with Jerusalem? What concord is there between the Academy and the Church? what between heretics and Christians? Our instruction comes from "the porch of Solomon," who had himself taught that "the Lord should be sought in simplicity of heart." Away with all attempts to produce a mottled Christianity of Stoic, Platonic, and dialectic composition! . . . For this is our [honorable] faith, that there is nothing which we ought to believe besides [the gospel]."[4]

In spite of his theological precision in some areas, Tertullian eventually joined the Montanist movement. His association with that movement has made him a somewhat controversial figure in subsequent church history.

❖ **For Discussion:** The doctrine of the Trinity is based on two fundamental truths: (1) There is only one God, and (2) one God eternally exists in three distinct Persons—Father, Son, and Holy Spirit—each of whom is truly and equally God. Can you think of some verses that would support these dual biblical truths?

## C. Origen of Alexandria (c. 184–253)

No survey of the Pre-Nicene church would be complete without mentioning Origen.

Origen was born in Alexandria, Egypt. As a young man, his father was martyred for being a Christian. Origen wanted to go with him to be martyred, but was prevented by his mother, who hid his clothes so he could not leave the house.

He attended a Christian training school in Alexandria, and was part of the church there until he came into conflict with the bishop. Origen moved to Caesarea, where he became a well-known teacher and prolific writer.

Origen was one of the most influential Christian thinkers of the early church, producing roughly ___2,000___ treatises on various theological subjects. His legacy, however, is a mix of both positive and negative contributions.

On the positive side, Origen organized the first systematic approach to theology in a work called *On First Principles*. He also wrote commentaries on a number of the books of the Bible, and defended the Christian faith against a pagan philosopher named Celsus.

On the negative side, Origen taught some strange doctrines, such as the pre-existence of the human soul.

He also promoted an allegorical approach to the interpretation of the Bible. The allegorical approach had already been used in Alexandria, and Origen continued to popularize it.

According to Origen's allegorical method, each text of Scripture has three levels of meaning, corresponding to the body, soul, and spirit.

- **The body:** the _____literal_____ meaning focused on what the text says if taken at face value. This meaning was regarded as the least helpful.

- **The soul:** the _____ethical_____ meaning involved the moral truth being taught by the text.

- **The spirit:** the _____spiritual_____ meaning allowed the interpreter to turn the text into a series of symbols or metaphors, which were generally interpreted in ways that pointed to Jesus.

Though Origen's allegorical approach to interpretation was undoubtedly well-intentioned, it opened the door to all sorts of imaginative and fanciful interpretations.

During the persecution of Christianity under Emperor Decius, Origen was tortured for his faith. Those injuries permanently damaged his health and he died several years later.

Because of some of Origen's controversial teachings, he was condemned by a sixth-century church council: the Second Council of Constantinople in 553.

❖ **For Discussion:** As noted above, Origen's approach to biblical interpretation left the door open for imaginative and fanciful interpretations that had nothing to do with the passage of Scripture being studied. Why is it important to have a sound method for studying and interpreting the Bible (see 2 Tim. 2:15)? What are some potential consequences for misinterpreting Scripture?

- In Lesson 6, we will look at a fourth-century preacher named John Chrysostom, who exhibited a much better approach to Bible interpretation. Chrysostom insisted that the meaning of a passage had to be tied to a literal understanding of the text. In this way, he avoided the problems that come with allegorizing God's Word.

## V. STANDING FOR TRUTH

The Christian leaders of the second and third centuries faced unique challenges.

Faithfulness to Christ required the courage to stand firm, even in the face of severe opposition, violent persecution, and possibly even execution. Men like Justin and Irenaeus gave their lives as martyrs for Christ, as did other believers during this time period. Their resolve did not waver even in the face of death.

Within the church, faithfulness to Christ also meant holding fast to the truth in the face of error. False teachers presented a constant threat. In response, church leaders wrote careful and convincing refutations, basing their arguments on the teaching of God's Word.

As we consider their examples, let's stop to consider what faithfulness to the Lord looks like in our lives—both inside and outside the church.

❖ **For Discussion:** How can believers in the church today continue to contend earnestly for the faith? What prevents believers from taking a strong stand in the areas of apologetics and polemics? What can you do to be faithful as a follower of Jesus Christ?

# Lesson 5

# DEFENDING THE DEITY OF CHRIST

Athanasius and the Council of Nicaea

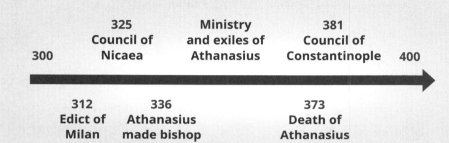

## I. A MAJOR TURNING POINT

Under Emperor Diocletian, Christians in the Roman Empire were intensely persecuted. For 250 years, going back to the time of Nero, believers in the Roman world faced intermittent waves of governmental persecution. But that was about to change.

After Diocletian's reign ended in 305, a power struggle ensued within the Roman Empire.

Several years later, Constantine I (the Great) gained control of the western Roman Empire by defeating Maximian in 310 and his son Maxentius in 312.

Prior to the battle with Maxentius, Constantine claimed to see a vision in which he was told to conquer in the sign of the cross. As a result of that experience, Constantine professed to become a Christian.

In 313, Constantine and Licinius (Roman Emperor in the east) issued the _____Edict of Milan,_____ which brought peace and legal protections to the Christian church. Followers of Jesus who lived in the Roman Empire went from being a persecuted people to a protected class.

In _____324,_____ Constantine defeated Licinius and became the sole ruler of the entire Roman Empire.

The next year, in 325, Constantine organized the first general church council (since the Jerusalem Council in Acts 15). The council met in Nicaea.

Later, under Theodosius the Great (who reigned from 379–395), Nicene Christianity was exclusively made the official religion of the Roman Empire.

## II. ATHANASIUS AND THE COUNCIL OF NICAEA

Athanasius lived in the fourth century (from around 298–373). He pastored the church in Alexandria, Egypt.

The central theological issue in Athanasius' day was the _____deity_____ of Jesus Christ, and the closely related doctrine of the Trinity.

Athanasius doggedly defended the deity of Christ. As a result, he was instrumental in keeping the church from falling into serious doctrinal error.

Some have called Athanasius "The Saint of Stubbornness," because he refused to compromise his defense of the truth.

Before becoming the bishop (or lead pastor) of the church in Alexandria, Athanasius served as a deacon, under the leadership of a man named Alexander.

One of the elders in the church, a man named Arius, began to teach that Christ was a created being who was not eternal and, therefore, not equal to God the Father.

Alexander condemned Arius for his heretical views, but Arius kept promoting his position.

The controversy resulted in a regional synod (held in Egypt in 318), and eventually led to the Council of Nicaea (involving church leaders throughout the entire Roman Empire) in 325.

The council was called by Roman Emperor Constantine, and its primary purpose was to resolve this controversy. Nearly 320 bishops from throughout the Roman Empire, and even some surrounding regions, traveled to Nicaea (accompanied by elders and deacons from their churches) to participate in the council. They understood the importance of the issue being debated.

Though Athanasius was only a deacon at the time of the council, his views were clearly represented by Alexander.

At the council, three primary positions on the deity of Christ were put forward:

▶ ___Hetero-ousios___ ("Of a Different Substance"): This was Arius's view. As noted above, he taught that Jesus Christ, the Son of God, was a created being. Thus, he argued, Jesus was of a different substance or essence from God the Father. On this basis, Arius contended that Christ was not equal in authority or deity with the Father. Put simply, Arius denied that Jesus is God, teaching instead that He is a creature.

▶ ___Homo-ousios___ ("Of the Same Substance"): In contrast to Arius, Alexander and Athanasius insisted that Jesus Christ was not a created being. Rather, He is the eternal Son of God who is co-equal to the Father. Because God the Son is eternal, just like the Father, He is of the same substance or essence as the Father. In other words, Alexander and Athanasius affirmed that Jesus is God, teaching that He is not a creature, but the uncreated Creator.

▶ ___Homoi-ousios___ ("Of a Similar Substance"): When the original position of Arius (hetero-ousios) was immediately rejected by the bishops attending the council, a modified version was put forward. It suggested that the Son of God was of a "similar substance" to the Father. Arius and his supporters shifted to this position, using the language of "similar substance" to minimize the differences they said existed between the Father and the Son. Alexander and Athanasius refused to accept this position because they rightly understood that "similar" still means "different."

After weeks of discussion, the council overwhelmingly affirmed the homo-ousios position, declaring their belief that the Son of God is "of the same substance" as God the Father. God the Son is co-eternal, co-essential, and co-equal with God the Father.

One interesting tradition suggests that a bishop named Nicholas of Myra (c. 270–343) attended the council. Incensed by Arius's denial of Jesus' deity, Nicholas got up during the proceedings, faced Arius, and slapped him in the face for blasphemy. Over time, Nicholas became known as "Saint Nicholas" and eventually, Santa Claus. Though the modern distortions of Santa Claus distract and detract from the worship of Jesus, it is remarkable to note that the original "Saint Nicholas" was a fervent defender of Christ's deity.

❖ **For Discussion:** What does it mean that God the Son is co-eternal with God the Father? Read John 1:1–3. How do these verses relate to what happened at the Council of Nicaea?

### III. THE STARTING PLACE: BIBLICAL AUTHORITY

Why did the Christian leaders who gathered in Nicaea overwhelmingly affirm the doctrine of Christ's deity? Their primary starting point was the Scriptures, and they saw this truth clearly taught in God's Word.

Along those lines, the fourth-century church leader Gregory of Nyssa (a younger contemporary of Athanasius) explained, in his conflict with the Arians, that Scripture alone must be the determiner of such things. No council or church tradition would suffice.

> **Gregory of Nyssa** (c. 335–395): "What then is our reply [to the Arians]? We do not think that it is right to make their prevailing custom the law and rule of sound doctrine. For if custom [or tradition] is to avail for proof of soundness, we too, surely, may advance our prevailing custom; and if they reject this, we are surely not bound to follow theirs. Let the inspired Scripture, then, be our umpire, and the vote of truth will surely be given to those whose dogmas are found to agree with the Divine words."[1]

In the same way we must look to God's Word as the *authoritative basis* for what we believe, Christian leaders of the first few centuries of church history similarly examined the Scriptures to see if these things were so (see Acts 17:11).

The truth of Jesus' deity permeates the Scriptures. Here are ten lines of evidence that affirm the doctrine of Christ's deity, with corresponding biblical references:

1. _____Divine Prophecy_____—In the Old Testament, the prophet Isaiah foretold that the Messiah would be "Mighty God" (Isa. 9:6; Matt. 1:23).

2. _____Divine Existence_____—Jesus explained that He was with the Father in eternity past, before the world began (John 17:5; see also John 1:1–2; 6:62; 8:23; 16:28).

3. _____The Divine Name_____—By calling Himself "I Am" in John 8:58, Jesus identified Himself as Yahweh, the covenant name for God in the Old Testament (see also John 6:51; 10:9, 11; 11:25; 14:6; 15:1). Other New Testament writers also take Old Testament texts about Yahweh and apply them directly to Jesus (see Matt. 3:3; Rom. 10:9–13; Phil. 2:10–11; 1 Peter 3:14–15).

4. _____Divine Authority_____—Jesus claimed authority over the Sabbath (Matt. 12:8; Mark 2:28; Luke 6:5) and over the ultimate destinies of people (John 8:24; see also Luke 12:8–9; John 5:22, 27–29). He also claimed the authority to forgive sins (Mark 2:5–11). Even Jesus' enemies recognized that this kind of authority belongs exclusively to God.

5. _____Divine Power_____—Jesus not only claimed divine authority, He exercised divine power. With nothing more than a word, He dominated demons (Mark 1:2–27; 3:11; 5:1–20), subdued nature (Luke 5:1–11; 8:22–25; 9:10–17), and eradicated disease (Mark 1:29–31, 40–45; 5:25–43; 8:22–26). He repeatedly exhibited the power to do what only God can do.

6. _____Divine Ownership_____—In keeping with His divine prerogative, Jesus claimed possession of that which belongs to God alone. He asserted that God's angels are His angels (Matt. 13:41; 24:30–31), that God's chosen people are His chosen people (Matt. 24:30–31), and that God's kingdom is His kingdom (Matt. 13:41; 16:28; Luke 1:33).

7. _____Divine Exaltation_____—The Old Testament forbids the worship of anyone but God alone (Ex. 20:3). Yet, the New Testament declares Jesus to be worthy of worship (Matt. 14:33; 28:9; Luke 24:53; Phil. 2:10–11; Heb. 1:6; Rev. 1:17). The clear implication is that Jesus is God.

8. _____Divine Titles_____—Jesus applied divine titles to Himself. For example, He called Himself the Son of Man, a title reflecting the divine implications of Daniel 7:13–14. He also called Himself the Son of God. Even His enemies recognized that by using that title, Jesus was claiming equality with God (Matt. 27:43; John 5:18; 10:46; 19:7).

9. _____Divine Unity_____—In the upper room on the night before His death, Jesus explained that He was in perfect unity with the Father. He told His disciples, "If you've seen Me, you've seen the Father" (John 14:9–10; see also 10:30; 12:45). If Jesus were not co-equal with the Father, He could never make such a claim and be telling the truth.

10. _____Divine Affirmation_____—The rest of the New Testament writings, beyond the four gospels, repeatedly affirm that Jesus is God. The collective evidence from the New Testament provides an insurmountable case for affirming the deity of Christ (John 1:1; Acts 20:28; Rom. 9:5; 1 Cor. 1:24; 2 Cor. 4:4; Phil. 2:6; Col. 2:9; Titus 2:13; Heb. 1:3, 8; 2 Peter 1:1; 1 John 5:20).

It should be noted that in passages like Colossians 1:15 where the word "firstborn" is used of Jesus, it does not mean that Jesus was the first created being. Instead, it refers to the fact that He stands in a position of prominence and preeminence over creation. In the ancient world, this understanding of "firstborn" was in keeping with the rights and privileges generally associated with being the oldest son. So when Paul says that Jesus is the "firstborn of all creation," he means that Jesus, as the Creator (v. 16), occupies the first place of highest honor over all creation.

That this is the intended meaning is made clear from v. 18, where Paul writes that Jesus is "the firstborn from the dead." Jesus was not the first person in human history to be resurrected from the dead (for example, see 1 Kings 17:17–24; 2 Kings 4:20–37; 2 Kings 13:21; Mark 5:35–43; Luke 7:11–17; John 11:1–44). But, He stands in a position of prominence and preeminence over anyone else who has been or will be raised. Thus, He is rightly regarded as the "firstborn," since He occupies the position of highest rank and honor.

Armed with the truth of God's Word, the pastors who attended the council of Nicaea agreed to uphold biblical truth. Conversely, they condemned the teachings of Arius as heretical and dangerous.

❖ **For Discussion:** Of the reasons listed above, which do you find most compelling regarding the deity of Christ? How would you use these reasons to present the truth that Jesus is God to an unbeliever?

## IV. THE WITNESS OF HISTORY: PATRISTIC AFFIRMATION

Because the council of Nicaea occurred in the year 325, the leaders who gathered there were also aware of the teachings of prior generations of Christians. Though not authoritative, these writings provided unmistakable testimony to the fact that believers from the first century onward worshiped Jesus Christ as God.

For example, around 106, the Roman governor Pliny the Younger wrote a letter in which he explained that the Christians in his region sang hymns "to Christ as to a god."[2]

That commitment to the deity of Christ is affirmed repeatedly by earlier church leaders. Here is a representative list from ten earlier Christian writers:

**Ignatius of Antioch** (c. 50–117): "For our God, Jesus the Christ, was conceived by Mary according to God's plan, both from the seed of David and of the Holy Spirit."[3]

**Ignatius** (again): "Wait expectantly for the one who is above time: the Eternal, the Invisible, who for our sake became visible; the Intangible, the Unsuffering, who for our sake suffered, who for our sake endured in every way."[4]

**Polycarp of Smyrna** (c. 69–155): "Now may the God and Father of our Lord Jesus Christ, and the eternal high priest himself, the Son of God Jesus Christ, build you up in faith and truth . . ., and to us with you, and to all those under heaven who will yet believe in our Lord and God Jesus Christ and in his Father who raised him from the dead."[5]

**Epistle of Barnabas** (c. 130): "If the Lord submitted to suffer for our souls, even though he is Lord of the whole world, to whom God said at the foundation of the world, 'Let us make humankind according to our image and likeness,' how is it, then, that he submitted to suffer at the hands of humans?"[6]

**Justin** (c. 100–165): "Permit me first to recount the prophecies, which I wish to do in order to prove that Christ is called both God and Lord of hosts."[7]

**Justin** (again): "Therefore these words testify explicitly that He [Jesus] is witnessed to by Him [the Father] who established these things, as deserving to be worshipped, as God and as Christ."[8]

**Tatian** (c. 110–172): "We do not act as fools, O Greeks, nor utter idle tales when we announce that God was born in the form of man."[9]

**Melito of Sardis** (died c. 180): "He that hung up the earth in space was Himself hanged up; He that fixed the heavens was fixed with nails; He that bore up the earth was borne up on a tree; the Lord of all was subjected to ignominy in a naked body—God put to death! . . . [I]n order that He might not be seen, the luminaries turned away, and the day became darkened—because they slew God, who hung naked on the tree. . . . This is He who made the heaven and the earth, and in the beginning, together with the Father, fashioned man; who was announced by means of the law and the prophets; who put on a bodily form in the Virgin; who was hanged upon the tree; who was buried in the earth; who rose from the place of the dead, and ascended to the height of heaven, and sitteth on the right hand of the Father."[10]

**Irenaeus of Lyons** (c. 120–202): "[Jesus Christ] is Himself in His own right, beyond all men who ever lived, God, and Lord, and King Eternal, and the Incarnate Word, proclaimed by all the prophets, the apostles, and by the Spirit Himself."[11]

**Irenaeus** (again): "Christ Jesus [is] our Lord, and God, and Savior, and King, according to the will of the invisible Father."[12]

**Irenaeus** (again): "Christ Himself, therefore, together with the Father, is the God of the living, who spoke to Moses, and who was also manifested to the fathers."[13]

**Irenaeus** (again): "He received testimony from all that He was very man, and that He was very God, from the Father, from the Spirit, from angels, from the creation itself, from men, from apostate spirits and demons."[14]

**Clement of Alexandria** (c. 150–215): "This Word, then, the Christ, the cause of both our being at first (for He was in God) and of our well-being, this very Word has now appeared as man, He alone being both, both God and man—the Author of all blessings to us; by whom we, being taught to live well, are sent on our way to life eternal. . . . The Word, who in the beginning bestowed on us life as Creator when He formed us, taught us to live well when He appeared as our Teacher; that as God He might afterwards conduct us to the life which never ends."[15]

**Tertullian** (c. 160–225): "For God alone is without sin; and the only man without sin is Christ, since Christ is also God."[16]

**Tertullian** (again): "Thus Christ is Spirit of Spirit, and God of God, as light of light is kindled. . . . That which has come forth out of God is at once God and the Son of God, and the two are one. In this way also, as He is Spirit of Spirit and God of God, He is made a second in manner of existence—in position, not in nature; and He did not withdraw from the original source, but went forth. This ray of God, then, as it was always foretold in ancient times, descending into a certain virgin, and made flesh in her womb, is in His birth God and man united."[17]

**Caius** (c. 180–217): "For who is ignorant of the books of Irenaeus and Melito, and the rest, which declare Christ to be God and man? All the psalms, too, and hymns of brethren, which have been written from the beginning by the faithful, celebrate Christ the Word of God, ascribing divinity to Him."[18]

As these examples demonstrate, believers from the beginning of the church recognized the truth about Jesus Christ: He is truly God and truly man, the one Mediator between God and men.

❖ **For Discussion:** Of the above quotes from pre-Nicene Christian leaders, which ones stood out to you? What did you find compelling about those statements?

## V. THE COUNCIL'S CONCLUSION: CREEDAL ARTICULATION

At the Council of Nicaea in 325, the true church arose to defend the deity of Christ from Arian attack.

The Council of Nicaea did not _____determine_____ or _____establish_____ the doctrine of Christ's deity. It rather _____affirmed_____ and _____defended_____ the doctrine that had always been taught by the church going back to the time of the apostles and being established in the Scriptures.

The affirmation of His deity was overwhelmingly recognized by those who participated in the Council of Nicaea. Of the roughly 320 bishops who attended the council, all but two signed the Nicene Creed. Both were ardent supporters of Arius.

The Nicene Creed is one of the most influential in church history. Here is the crux of the Creed:

"We believe in one God, the Father Almighty, maker of all things visible and invisible; and in one Lord Jesus Christ, the Son of God, the only-begotten of His Father, of the substance of the Father, God of God, Light of Light, very God of very God, begotten, not made, being of one substance with the Father. By whom all things were made, both which are in heaven and in earth. Who for us men and for our salvation came down from heaven and was incarnate and was made man. He suffered and the third day He rose again, and ascended into heaven. And He shall come again to judge both the living and the dead. And we believe in the Holy Spirit."[19]

Half a century later, at the First Council of Constantinople (in 381), the Nicene Creed would be expanded to include more detail on the person and work of the Holy Spirit.

Though the victory at Nicaea had been overwhelming, the controversy with Arianism still raged in the Roman Empire over the next fifty years.

❖ **For Discussion:** Earlier in this lesson, we noted that the authority for what we believe must be the Bible, not a church council. Why is that principle important to remember, especially when studying the Council of Nicaea and the Nicene Creed?

## VI. STANDING AGAINST THE WORLD

Though he was only a deacon at the time of the Council of Nicaea (325), Athanasius spent most of the fourth century fighting the false teachings of Arius. He became the bishop of Alexandria just a few years later (in 328).

Over the next forty-five years of his ministry, he would be exiled five times, totaling seventeen years.

Despite being denounced at the Council of Nicaea, Arianism continued to be a popular view in the Roman Empire. As a result, Athanasius repeatedly found himself in the political crosshairs of his enemies.

► In 336, Athanasius was falsely accused of kidnapping another bishop (named Arsenius) and cutting off his hand for use in magical incantations.

► Although he was able to prove his innocence, he was still sent into exile (by Emperor Constantine) when his opponents accused him of interfering with wheat shipments from Alexandria to Rome. He was able to return to Alexandria two years later when Constantine died.

► A short time later, a supporter of Arius convinced Constantius II (Constantine's son) to get rid of Athanasius. This resulted in the next two exiles of Athanasius (from 339–346 and from 356–361).

► On one of those occasions, Roman soldiers stormed the church during a communion service, forcing Athanasius to flee and go into hiding in the Egyptian desert.

► In 362, Athanasius was again forced into exile by Emperor Julian. Unlike Constantine, Julian did not claim to be a Christian. He attempted to take the Roman Empire back into paganism. When it became obvious that Athanasius was resolute in his Christian conviction, Julian drove him out of Alexandria. The exile ended when Julian died.

► The fifth and final exile occurred under Emperor Valens who simply evicted Athanasius because he had been earlier exiled by Julian. When Valens realized that the people of Alexandria loved Athanasius, he had him restored to his office (in order to garner popularity with the citizens of Alexandria).

During these times of exile, it sometimes seemed like Athanasius was alone in his fight for the doctrine of Christ's deity. It seemed like it was Athanasius against the world. Yet, he refused to waiver in his commitment to the truth.

The reality is that others joined in the cause with Athanasius, including fourth-century leaders like Basil of Caesarea, Gregory of Nyssa, and Gregory of Nazianzus.

On a human level, their faithfulness was rewarded in 380, when Emperor Theodosius I outlawed the heretical views of Arius and declared Nicene (Trinitarian) Christianity to be the official religion of the Roman Empire.

❖ **For Discussion:** Athanasius endured 17 years of exile because he refused to compromise on the truth that Jesus is God. Why did Athanasius see the doctrine of the deity of Christ as so important? What would you be willing to go into exile for?

## VII. THE LEGACY OF ATHANASIUS

Here are a few lessons we can learn from the man nicknamed "the saint of stubbornness":

**We should be willing to contend earnestly for core Christian doctrines (see Jude 3–4).** A right understanding of the person of Christ is not peripheral but central to the faith. Athanasius recognized the importance of that truth, and he was willing to sacrifice much to defend it.

**At times, being faithful means you will also be unpopular.** Athanasius became the object of political attack and public scorn because he refused to compromise. His tenacity provides a compelling example for us to consider.

**The key to honoring God is to hold firmly and faithfully to what the Bible teaches.** The pastors who signed the Nicene Creed did so because they saw the deity of Christ clearly taught in Scripture. That same Bible-based conviction fueled the dogged determination of Athanasius, even in the face of great opposition.

**The examples of faithful men in generations past should motivate us to stand faithfully *against the world* in our own generation.** Athanasius lived out his convictions with constancy and courage. His commitment to the truth did not waver. His example should motivate us to do the same in our day. Biblical truth is constantly under attack. The question is, are we willing to stand for what we know is right and true?

❖ **For Discussion:** Which of these lessons is most compelling to you? What can you do to put that principle into practice?

# Lesson 6

# GRACE AND TRUTH
## Augustine, Chrysostom, and the Post-Nicene Church

**KEY PASSAGE: John 1:14–17**

*"And the Word became flesh, and dwelt among us, and we saw His glory, glory as of the only begotten from the Father, full of grace and truth. John testified about Him and cried out, saying, 'This was He of whom I said, "He who comes after me has a higher rank than I, for He existed before me."' For of His fullness we have all received, and grace upon grace. For the Law was given through Moses; grace and truth were realized through Jesus Christ."*

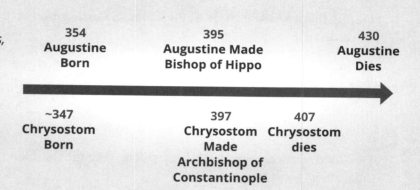

| 354 Augustine Born | 395 Augustine Made Bishop of Hippo | 430 Augustine Dies |
| --- | --- | --- |
| ~347 Chrysostom Born | 397 Chrysostom Made Archbishop of Constantinople | 407 Chrysostom dies |

## I. INTRODUCTION

This lesson will focus on two key tenets of the Christian faith: the grace of the gospel and the truth of God's Word. As the passage above demonstrates, both grace and truth were fully realized in the Lord Jesus.

In order to highlight these themes, we will consider the impact of two influential Christian leaders who lived in the late-fourth and early-fifth centuries.

Within the Roman Empire, one was from the West, the other from the East. One is known primarily as a theologian, though he was also a preacher. The other is known primarily as a preacher, though he also engaged in doctrinal discussion and debate.

The impact of their legacy reverberated in the centuries after them, and is still felt today. For Protestant Reformers like John Calvin (1509–1564), these two church fathers held a unique place of influence.

Calvin especially appreciated the theology of Augustine: his emphasis on man's sinful depravity and God's undeserved grace. Calvin also greatly valued the way Chrysostom approached the Bible, interpreting it in a straightforward way that explained the literal meaning of the text and emphasized its practical implications.

## II. AUGUSTINE (354–430)

Aurelius Augustinus ("Augustine") was born in North Africa, not far from the Mediterranean coast, in modern-day Algeria.

His father was an unbeliever, but his mother, Monica, was a Christian. She taught her son about the Bible and the Christian faith. She also prayed diligently for her son's conversion.

In his *Confessions*, Augustine explains how God saved him. In chapter 1, he famously prays, "Our hearts are restless until they find rest in You, Lord." The restlessness in Augustine's unredeemed heart compelled him to chase after the pleasures of this world.

At age sixteen, Augustine left home to study rhetoric in Carthage. A year later, he began a nearly fifteen-year romantic relationship with a woman whom he never married. Together, they had a son.

Augustine's search for satisfaction led him on a quest for truth. At this time, he rejected the Bible because he did not find it to be eloquent or philosophically sophisticated. Instead, he was attracted to the false teachings of Manichaeism—a heresy that attempted to combine Christianity with the false religion of Zoroastrianism.

During this time, Augustine was teaching in Carthage, but in 384, after a short stint in Rome, he acquired a teaching position in Milan.

By the time he came to Milan, he had abandoned Manichaeism and began to explore Neo-Platonism. But the longing he felt in his soul was still not satisfied.

In Milan, he went to hear the famous preacher Ambrose (340-397). As a teacher of rhetoric, Augustine went to listen to great oratory. But the content of Ambrose's sermons began to penetrate his heart.

God used the preaching of Ambrose, along with the testimony of some of Augustine's friends, to draw Augustine's heart to Himself.

One day, while sitting outside under a tree, he heard a child from a nearby house say, "Pick it up and read it." Augustine took this as if it came from God. He found a Bible and opened it. His eyes fell on the truth of Romans 13:13–14:

> **Romans 13:13–14**—"Let us behave properly as in the day, not in carousing and drunkenness, not in sexual promiscuity and sensuality, not in strife and jealousy. But put on the Lord Jesus Christ, and make no provision for the flesh in regard to its lusts."

When he read that passage, the blinders were removed from Augustine's eyes. He understood the gospel and believed.

After his conversion, Augustine initially desired a life of monastic contemplation and devotion to Christ. He was ordained as a priest in the year 391 by the church in Hippo Regius (modern day Annaba, Algeria).

In 395, the elderly bishop of Hippo appointed Augustine to serve as a co-bishop. He would serve as the bishop there until his death in 430.

In addition to preaching, Augustine wrote numerous treatises, including important theological works (like *On the Trinity* and *The City of God*), and important polemical works against heretical movements like Manichaeism and Pelagianism.

For Christians wanting to learn more about Augustine's life, his *Confessions* recounts the testimony of God's grace in saving him from a life of unrestrained sin.

Importantly, Augustine would become one of the most influential theologians in all of church history, especially in the West. As noted above, his writings made a significant impact on the Reformers during the sixteenth-century Protestant Reformation.

❖ **For Discussion:** Augustine's conversion story is admittedly dramatic. The reality is that every testimony of God's grace is amazing. With that in mind, how would you explain the way God rescued you from sin and drew you to Himself?

## A. Augustine and Grace

Augustine has been called __"The Doctor of Grace"__ because of his emphasis on God's grace in salvation.

This theme was especially prominent in his response to a false teacher named Pelagius. Pelagius taught that people are born morally neutral; they are therefore capable of pursuing God and obtaining salvation through their own volition and effort.

In response, Augustine insisted that people enter this world with a sinful nature (Ps. 51:5); they are spiritually dead in their sins (Eph. 2:1–3). They are therefore unable to earn God's favor through their own efforts. Rather, He must draw them to Himself and save them by His grace. God's saving grace is something that cannot be earned through personal merit or good works (Eph. 2:4–9).

Consider the following excerpts from Augustine's writings that highlight the theme of God's grace and mercy:

▶ Sinners are not justified on the basis of their own __merit.__ They are saved by __grace__ :

**Augustine:** "We conclude that a man is not justified by the precepts of a holy life, but by faith in Jesus Christ; in a word, not by the law of works, but by the law of faith; not by the letter, but by the spirit; not by the merits of deeds, but by free grace."[1]

**Augustine:** "No one merits justification by his good works, since unless he has been justified he cannot do good works. Nevertheless, God justifies the Gentiles by faith."[2]

▶ Old Testament saints, likewise, were not saved on the basis of their good works, but rather through __faith in Christ__ :

**Augustine:** "[Abraham] was justified not by his own merit, as if by works, but by the grace of God through faith."[3]

**Augustine:** [Speaking of Old Testament saints] "Of whatever virtue you may declare that the ancient righteous people were possessed, nothing saved them but the belief in the Mediator who shed his blood for the remission of their sins."[4]

▶ Because salvation is by grace and not by works, even the worst of sinners can be saved:

**Augustine:** "But what about the person who does no work? Think here of some godless sinner, who has no good works to show. What of him or her? What if such a person comes to believe in God who justifies the impious [namely, the ungodly]? . . . When someone believes in him who justifies the impious, that faith is reckoned as justice to the believer, as David too declares that person blessed whom God has accepted and endowed with righteousness, independently of any righteous actions. What righteousness is this? The righteousness of faith, preceded by no good works, but with good works as its consequence."[5]

**Augustine:** "There is another sense in this verse, 'For nothing You will save them:' with none of their merits going before You will save them. . . . All in them is rough, all foul, all to be detested: and though they bring nothing to You whereby they may be saved; 'For nothing You will save them,' that is, with the free gift of Your grace."[6]

▶ The gospel of grace precludes anyone from boasting about their salvation:

>**Augustine:** "The people who boast imagine that they are justified by their own efforts, and therefore they glory in themselves, not in the Lord."[7]

>**Augustine:** "No man can say that it is by the merit of his own works, or by the merit of his own prayers, or by the merit of his own faith, that God's grace has been conferred upon him; nor suppose that the doctrine is true which those heretics hold, that the grace of God is given us in proportion to our own merit."[8]

Augustine did not always speak about justification with the kind of consistency or clarity of the sixteenth-century Protestant Reformers.[9] Nonetheless, as the above examples demonstrate, he clearly affirmed the truth of Ephesians 2:8–10:

>**Ephesians 2:8–10**—"For by grace you have been saved through faith; and that not of yourselves, it is the gift of God; not as a result of works, so that no one may boast. For we are His workmanship, created in Christ Jesus for good works, which God prepared beforehand so that we would walk in them."

❖ **For Discussion:** "Mercy" refers to the withholding of a deserved punishment. "Grace" refers to the reception of an undeserved blessing. In salvation, God extends both mercy and grace to us. What do Christians deserve that they will not receive? What will they receive that they do not deserve?

## B. Augustine and Truth

In addition to emphasizing the fact that salvation is by grace alone, Augustine also declared his allegiance and submission to the Word of Truth, the Bible.

Augustine recognized that, because it comes from God, Scripture is free from error. To state that another way, Augustine affirmed that the Bible is absolutely true:

>**Augustine:** "I have learned to yield this respect and honor only to the canonical books of Scripture: of these alone do I most firmly believe that the authors were completely free from error."[10]

>**Augustine:** "The Scriptures are holy, they are truthful, they are blameless."[11]

>**Augustine:** "It seems to me that most disastrous consequences must follow upon our believing that anything false is found in the sacred books."[12]

Augustine not only viewed Scripture as inerrant (without error), but also as absolute in its authority. There is no authority higher than the Word of God:

>**Augustine:** "This Mediator, having spoken what He judged sufficient first by the prophets, then by His own lips, and afterwards by the apostles, has besides produced the Scripture which is called canonical, which has paramount authority, and to which we yield assent in all matters of which we ought not to be ignorant, and yet cannot know of ourselves."[13]

>**Augustine:** "Therefore everything written in Scripture must be believed absolutely."[14]

As a result, Augustine saw the Bible as a higher authority than anything else ever written, including the writings of earlier church fathers.[15]

> **Augustine:** "In the innumerable books that have been written after [the close of the canon] we may sometimes find the same truth as in Scripture, but there is not the same authority. Scripture has a sacredness peculiar to itself."[16]

Recognizing the Bible's authority, Augustine taught that any dispute related to doctrine or the church should be resolved by appealing to the truth of Scripture:

> **Augustine:** "Let those things be removed from our midst which we quote against each other not from divine canonical books but from elsewhere. Someone may perhaps ask: Why do you want to remove these things from the midst? Because I do not want the holy church proved by human documents but by divine oracles."[17]

> **Augustine:** "Let us not hear: This I say, this you say; but thus says the Lord. Surely it is the books of the Lord on whose authority we both agree and which we both believe. There let us seek the church, there let us discuss our case."[18]

Augustine understood that even the authority of church councils, like the Council of Nicaea, must be subjected to the authority of Scripture. His comment to a proponent of Arianism makes that clear:

> **Augustine:** "I must not press the authority of Nicaea against you, nor you that of Ariminum against me; I do not acknowledge the one, as you do not the other; but let us come to ground that is common to both, the testimony of the Holy Scriptures."[19]

Importantly, Augustine also saw the Bible as sufficient—meaning that the Word of God reveals the truth necessary to know sound doctrine and live righteously (2 Tim. 3:16–17):

> **Augustine:** "For among the things that are plainly laid down in Scripture are to be found all matters that concern faith and the manner of life."[20]

> **Augustine:** "What more shall I teach you than what we read in the apostle? For holy Scripture fixes the rule of our doctrine, lest we be wiser than we ought. . . . Therefore, let it not be for me to teach you any other thing except to expound to you the words of the [divine] Teacher, and to treat them as the Lord will have given to me."[21]

A millennium after Augustine, the Protestant Reformers rallied around these same convictions: that the Word of God is inerrant, authoritative, and sufficient. Though the Reformers did not agree with Augustine on every theological nuance, they greatly appreciated his emphasis on the undeserved nature of God's grace and the authoritative truth of God's Word.

❖ **For Discussion:** Read 2 Timothy 3:16–17. Those verses highlight the inspiration, authority, and sufficiency of Scripture. What does it mean that the Bible is sufficient? What are the practical implications of that reality?

## III. JOHN CHRYSOSTOM (C. 347–407)

John was born in the city of Antioch, around the year 347. As a young man, he was trained in rhetoric, and excelled in oratory.

In his zeal to serve the Lord, John left Antioch to live as a monk in the wilderness. During these two years, he spent the majority of his time committing Scripture to memory. He lived in harsh conditions, getting minimal food and rest. As a result, he damaged his health, and had to return to the city.

Back in Antioch, John began to preach in the main church there. In his *homilies* (or sermons), he taught through the New Testament going verse by verse through the text. He interpreted the Bible literally rather than allegorically, and was careful to draw out the practical implications of the text for his listeners.

The style and substance of his preaching made him very popular with the people in Antioch. The name "Chrysostom" means _____"Golden Mouth."_____ Indeed, John Chrysostom is one of the most famous preachers in church history.

In 397, he was appointed the bishop of Constantinople, having been nominated by a friend without his knowledge.

Constantinople was the capital city of the eastern Roman Empire. As Chrysostom preached against the flaunting of wealth, he came into conflict with the Empress—who thought John was targeting her in his sermons.

That conflict, among other things, resulted in Chrysostom being exiled from Constantinople. He died in the year 407, while in exile.

❖ **For Discussion:** As a Christian, Chrysostom committed himself to meditating on and memorizing large portions of the Bible. Read Psalm 119:11, 105. Why is it important for believers to hide God's Word in their hearts?

## A. Chrysostom and Grace

Because John was so carefully tied to the biblical text, his preaching in many places affirms that salvation is by grace through faith alone.

For the following examples, look up the New Testament passage on which John Chrysostom is commenting. Then, as you read Chrysostom's comment, take note of his emphasis on salvation by grace through faith, apart from works.

1. **Chrysostom on Romans 3:27**: "But what is the 'law of faith?' It is, being saved by grace. Here he shows God's power, in that He has not only saved, but has even justified, and led them to boasting, and this too without needing works, but looking for faith only."[22]

2. **Chrysostom on Romans 5:2**: "If then He has brought us near to Himself, when we were far off, much more will He keep us now that we are near. And let me beg you to consider how He everywhere sets down these two points; His part, and our part. On His part, however, there be things varied and numerous and diverse. For He died for us, and further reconciled us, and brought us to Himself, and gave us grace unspeakable. But we brought faith only as our contribution."[23]

3. **Chrysostom on Ephesians 2:8**: "Even faith, [Paul] says, is not from us. For if the Lord had not come, if He had not called us, how should we have been able to believe? 'For how,' [Paul] says, 'shall they believe if they have not heard?' (Rom. 10:14). So even the act of faith is not self-initiated. It is, he says, 'the gift of God'"[24]

4. **Chrysostom on Colossians 1:26–28**: "To have brought humanity, more senseless than stones, to the dignity of angels simply through bare words, and faith alone, without any hard work, is indeed a rich and glorious mystery. It is just as if one were to take a dog, quite consumed with hunger and the mange, foul and loathsome to see, and not so much as able to move but lying passed out, and make him all at once into a human being and to display him upon the royal throne."[25]

5. **Chrysostom on 1 Timothy 1:15–16**: "For as people, on receiving some great good, ask themselves if it is not a dream, as not believing it; so it is with respect to the gifts of God. What then was it that was thought incredible? That those who were enemies and sinners, justified by neither the law nor works, should immediately through faith alone be advanced to the highest favor. . . . It seemed to them incredible that a person who had misspent all his former life in vain and wicked actions should afterwards be saved by his faith alone. On this account he [Paul] says, 'It is a saying to be believed.'"[26]

In these excerpts, Chrysostom clearly expresses the truth of the gospel of grace. His clarity is due to the fact that he was looking to the Word of God and interpreting its truth in a straightforward way.

For Christians today, our understanding of the gospel must also be grounded in the text of God's Word.

❖ **For Discussion:** Of the biblical passages listed above, where would you start if you were explaining the gospel to someone who is not a Christian?

## B. Chrysostom and Truth

Like Augustine, Chrysostom affirmed that God's Word is without error. Commenting on John 17:17, he said:

> **Chrysostom:** "'Your word is truth,' that is, 'there is no falsehood in it, and all that is said in it must happen.'"[27]

Chrysostom also affirmed the authority of Scripture, noting that all arguments must be supported from the Word of God:

> **Chrysostom:** "These then are the reasons; but it is necessary to establish them all from the Scriptures, and to show with exactness that all that has been said on this subject is not an invention of human reasoning, but the very sentence of the Scriptures. For thus will what we say be at once more deserving of credit, and sink the deeper into your minds."[28]

Likewise, he affirmed the sufficiency of Scripture. Commenting on 2 Timothy 3:16–17, he declares:

> **Chrysostom:** "For this is the exhortation of the Scripture given, that the man of God may be rendered perfect by it; without this therefore he cannot be perfect. You have the Scriptures, he says, in place of me. If you would learn anything, you may learn it from them. And if he thus wrote to Timothy, who was filled with the Spirit, how much more to us!"[29]

One important point to add regarding Chrysostom has to do with his method of interpreting the Bible. Rather than treating the biblical accounts like allegories, as Origen did, Chrysostom took the Bible at face value. He interpreted it in a literal way.

**Chrysostom:** "For we ought to unlock the passage by first giving a clear interpretation of the words. What then does the saying mean? . . . We must not attend to the words merely, but turn our attention to the sense, and learn the aim of the speaker, and the cause and the occasion, and by putting all these things together turn out the hidden meaning."[30]

As Chrysostom explains, proper Bible interpretation involves a clear understanding of what the passage means. Sound Bible study involves looking at details like the _____words,_____ the flow of the argument _____in its context_____ (the sense), the author's _____intent_____ (the aim of the speaker), and the _____historical setting_____ (the cause and the occasion).

It is encouraging to see a notable preacher from history practicing these principles all the way back in the fourth century.

❖ **For Discussion:** In Lesson 4, we learned about Origen's allegorical approach to Bible interpretation. How was Chrysostom's approach different? Why is it a better way to approach the study of God's Word?

## IV. PUTTING IT ALL TOGETHER

Much more could be said about both Augustine and Chrysostom, not to mention other leaders in the Post-Nicene period.

The goal of this lesson was to highlight the commitment expressed by these early Christian leaders to (a) the gospel of grace, and (b) the Word of truth.

As has been noted, these convictions resonated with the Protestant Reformers in the sixteenth century.

For the Reformers, the gospel of grace was expressed as follows: sinners are justified by "grace alone" through "faith alone" in the person and work of "Christ alone."

Their commitment to the authority and sufficiency of Scripture is similarly captured by the phrase, "Scripture alone." We will explore those themes in more detail in Lesson 10.

Evangelical Christians can rejoice in seeing a clear testimony to these foundational truths from two of church history's leading voices, dating back to the fourth and fifth centuries.

❖ **For Discussion:** What would happen if the church were to either (a) ignore the authority of God's Word, or (b) lose sight of the true gospel? What can Christians do to safeguard these core doctrines?

# PART III

# THE MIDDLE AGES

6$^{TH}$–15$^{TH}$ CENTURIES

# Lesson 7
# CONTROVERSIES AND COUNCILS
## Doctrinal Debates in the Late Patristic Period and Early Middle Ages

**KEY PASSAGE: 2 John 9**

*"Anyone who goes too far and does not abide in the teaching of Christ, does not have God; the one who abides in the teaching, he has both the Father and the Son."*

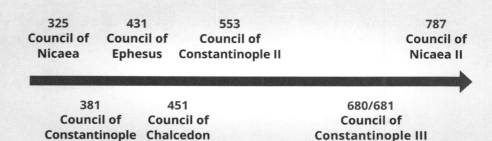

| 325 Council of Nicaea | 431 Council of Ephesus | 553 Council of Constantinople II | | 787 Council of Nicaea II |

| | 381 Council of Constantinople | 451 Council of Chalcedon | 680/681 Council of Constantinople III | |

## I. CONTENDING FOR THE TRUTH

The New Testament predicts the coming of false teachers, who seek to undermine the truth and distort sound doctrine from within the church.

In **Matthew 7:15**, Jesus warned: "Beware of the false prophets, who come to you in sheep's clothing, but inwardly are ravenous wolves."

In **Acts 20:28–31**, the apostle Paul similarly instructed the Ephesian elders: "Be on guard for yourselves and for all the flock . . . I know that after my departure savage wolves will come in among you, not sparing the flock; . . . speaking perverse things, to draw away the disciples after them. Therefore be on the alert."

Peter told his readers this in **2 Peter 2:1**, "But false prophets also arose among the people, just as there will also be false teachers among you, who will secretly introduce destructive heresies, even denying the Master who bought them, bringing swift destruction upon themselves."

In **2 John 7**, the apostle John explained that, "Many deceivers have gone out into the world, those who do not acknowledge Jesus Christ as coming in the flesh. This is the deceiver and the antichrist."

And **Jude 4** warns about "certain persons [who] have crept in unnoticed, those who were long beforehand marked out for this condemnation, ungodly persons who turn the grace of our God into licentiousness and deny our only Master and Lord, Jesus Christ."

As errors arose in the early centuries of church history, the true church responded by defending what Scripture teaches and clearly articulating the truth in the face of heretical attack.

After Emperor Constantine brought peace to Christians living in the Roman Empire (in the early fourth century), church leaders were able to address the major heresies of their day by organizing _____ synods _____ and _____ councils. _____

The largest of these councils were organized by the emperors themselves, and involved church leaders from all over the Roman world. These councils are known as _____ "ecumenical" _____ councils, because they included all of the churches in the empire.

71

In church history, Seven Ecumenical Councils are generally recognized. The central theological issues addressed at these seven councils centered on the Person of Jesus Christ.

In this lesson, we will focus on the three most important of these seven councils: the Council of Nicaea in 325, the First Council of Constantinople in 381, and the Council of Chalcedon in 451. The other four councils will be summarized briefly at the end.

❖ **For Discussion:** Read 2 John 7–11. In that passage, what was the primary doctrinal issue that the false teachers were distorting? Why is it so important to make sure that we have an accurate understanding of the Person of Jesus Christ?

## II. THE COUNCIL OF NICAEA (325)

Key Issue: _____The deity of Christ_____

Context:

▶ See earlier lesson on Athanasius in Lesson 5 for full context.

▶ Nearly 320 bishops gathered in Nicaea, at the invitation of Emperor Constantine. The Council lasted more than _____40_____ days.

▶ In addition to addressing the doctrinal issue of Christ's deity, the Council also addressed the date for celebrating _____Resurrection Sunday (Easter)._____

Positions:

▶ Hetero-ousios ("Of a Different Substance")—This was Arius's view. As noted in Lesson 5, he taught that Jesus Christ, the Son of God, was a created being. Thus, he argued, Jesus was of a different substance or essence than God the Father. On this basis, Arius contended that Christ was not equal in authority or deity with the Father. Put simply, Arius denied that Jesus is God, teaching instead that He is a creature.

▶ Homo-ousios ("Of the Same Substance")—In contrast to Arius, Alexander and Athanasius insisted that Jesus Christ was not a created being. Rather, He is the eternal Son of God who is co-equal to the Father. Because God the Son is eternal, just like the Father, He is of the same substance or essence as the Father. In other words, Alexander and Athanasius affirmed that Jesus is God, teaching that He is not a creature, but the uncreated Creator.

▶ Homoi-ousios ("Of a Similar Substance")—When Arius's original position (hetero-ousios) was rejected, a modified version was put forward. It suggested that the Son of God was of a "similar substance" to the Father. Arius and his supporters shifted to this position, using the language of "similar substance" to minimize the differences they said existed between the Father and the Son. Alexander and Athanasius refused to accept this position because they rightly understood that "similar" still means "different."

Results:

▶ The views of Arius were rejected by the council. The Nicene Creed, which was adopted by the Council, defended the truth that God the Son is co-eternal, co-essential, and co-equal with God the Father.

► Here is the main part of the Nicene Creed:

**The Nicene Creed:** "We believe in one God, the Father Almighty, maker of all things visible and invisible; and in one Lord Jesus Christ, the Son of God, the only begotten of His Father, of the substance of the Father, God of God, Light of Light, very God of very God, begotten, not made, being of one substance with the Father. By whom all things were made, both which are in heaven and in earth. Who for us men and for our salvation came down from heaven and was incarnate and was made man. He suffered and the third day He rose again, and ascended into heaven. And He shall come again to judge both the living and the dead. And we believe in the Holy Spirit."[1]

► The Creed continues by noting that the "catholic" church affirms this truth. It is important to explain that, at this time in history, the term "catholic" simply meant "universal." It did not refer to the later Roman Catholic church.

► The Creed focuses on the deity of Christ, because that was the primary issue at stake. Although it affirms belief in the Holy Spirit, it does not explain the doctrine of the Holy Spirit in any detail.

❖ **For Discussion:** Read John 1:1, 5:18, and 8:58–59. How should those verses inform our thinking about the Council of Nicaea? What do those passages teach about the equality (to the Father) and eternality of God the Son?

## III. THE FIRST COUNCIL OF CONSTANTINOPLE (381)

Key Issues:  <u>     The deity and humanity of Christ     </u>

<u>          The deity of the Holy Spirit          </u>

Context:

► In spite of the Nicene Creed, the false teachings of Arius continued to be very popular in the Roman Empire. The view of homoiousios (that the Son of God is of a "similar," but still different, substance than the Father) was particularly popular.

► Athanasius, along with other church leaders like Basil of Caesarea (c. 329–379), Gregory of Nyssa (c. 335–c. 395), and Gregory of Nazianzus (c. 329–390), continued to defend the doctrine of Christ's equality to the Father.

► In rejecting the doctrine of the Trinity, the followers of Arius also denied the deity of the Holy Spirit. Proponents of this view were known as the Pneumatomachians, which means "combaters against the Spirit." Basil of Caesarea refuted their views in his work, On the Holy Spirit.

► A new heresy about Christ called Apollinarianism also arose. The creator of this view (Apollinaris of Laodicea) taught that although Jesus possessed a human body, He did not have a human spirit/soul. Instead, His physical body was like a shell occupied by a divine mind.

► These issues motivated Emperor Theodosius I (d. 395) to convene a council in Constantinople in 381. The council lasted for three months.

Positions:

- ▸ _____Arianism_____—Advocates of the Arian position held to a "homoiousios" view of Jesus' nature. They contended that although the Son of God possessed a "similar nature" to God the Father, He did not possess the "same nature." They came to this conclusion because they denied the eternality of the Son, arguing instead that He was a created being.

- ▸ _____Apollinarianism_____—Although Apollinaris affirmed the deity of Christ, he did not accept the full humanity of Christ. Instead, he saw Jesus' human body as the physical shell in which His divine mind dwelt. His deity was like a letter being placed inside the envelope of His humanity. Thus, Apollinaris denied that Jesus possessed a human soul.

- ▸ _____Trinitarianism_____—The orthodox position insisted that the incarnate Christ is both truly God and truly man. Hence, He possessed both a full divine nature and a full human nature. Moreover, with regard to the Holy Spirit, the orthodox position affirmed the full deity of the Spirit of God. The Trinity consists of three co-equal Persons: Father, Son, and Holy Spirit.

Results:

- ▸ The Council affirmed the Nicene Creed.

- ▸ Both Arianism and Apollinarianism were denounced as heretical positions. In so doing, the Council affirmed a belief in both the full deity and full humanity of Christ.

- ▸ In an effort to defend the deity of the Holy Spirit, the Council expanded the Nicene Creed to be explicit in its affirmation of the Holy Spirit as the Third Member of the Trinity.

- ▸ Here is the expanded section regarding the Holy Spirit that this Council added to the Nicene Creed:

  > **Expanded Section of the Nicene-Constantinopolitan Creed:** "We believe in the Holy Spirit, the Lord and Giver of Life, who proceeds from the Father [and the Son], who is to be worshipped and glorified with the Father and the Son, and who spoke through the prophets."[2]

- ▸ The phrase "and the Son" is included in brackets because it was not part of the original, Greek version of the Creed. Instead, it was added later by the western church to the Latin version of the Creed. This addition eventually led to controversy between the eastern and western halves of the Roman church.

❖ **For Discussion:** Apollinarianism denied the full (or true) humanity of Christ. Read Hebrews 4:14–16. Why is it so important that our Mediator be truly human? See also Romans 5:12–21.

## IV. THE COUNCIL OF CHALCEDON (451)

Key Issue: _____The two natures of Christ (His deity and His humanity)_____

Context:

- ▸ The Council of Constantinople had affirmed the true deity and true humanity of Jesus Christ. The eternal Son of God, the Second Member of the Trinity, took on flesh and became a man in His incarnation (Phil. 2:6–7).

- But questions remained as to how those two natures (the divine and the human) related to one another in the person of Jesus Christ. This question would be addressed at the Council of Chalcedon.

- Emperor Marcian called the council. He had denounced an earlier council that met in Ephesus in 449 as being illegitimate. The Council of Chalcedon was convened to override it.

- Some 370 bishops attended. Leo I (bishop of Rome from 440–461) was unable to attend, but sent a letter (called his Tome) to be read at the Council. The content of Leo's Tome was approved by the Council as articulating the orthodox position.

The Positions:

- _____ Nestorianism _____—This view divided the two natures of Christ, putting a wall of separation between them to the point that He was viewed as two persons. There is debate as to whether Nestorius (the archbishop of Constantinople from 428–431) actually held the view associated with his name. In summary, Nestorianism asserted that Christ possessed two natures and was therefore two persons.

- _____ Eutychianism _____—In response to Nestorianism, Eutyches emphasized that Jesus Christ was a single person with a single divine nature. The human nature was either eclipsed by the divine nature, or mixed together with the divine resulting in a hybrid nature. In summary, Eutychianism argued that Christ was only one person and therefore possessed only one nature.

- _____ Hypostatic Union _____—Leo articulated a position that avoided the errors of both Nestorianism and Eutychianism. He affirmed that Christ, in His incarnation, possesses two natures (divine and human). If Jesus is both truly God and truly man, the integrity of each nature must be preserved. Yet, at the same time, Leo also affirmed that Christ is a single person. In becoming a man, Jesus did not become multiple persons. In summary, Leo's position asserted that Christ is a single person who possesses two natures.

The Result:

- Leo's position was affirmed by the Council as being biblical and the historic position of the church.

- The writings of Eutyches and his followers were condemned.

- The Council produced a creed to articulate the orthodox position:

  **Chalcedonian Creed:** "Following the holy Fathers, we unanimously teach and confess one and the same Son, our Lord Jesus Christ: the same perfect in divinity and perfect in humanity, the same truly God and truly man, composed of rational soul and body; consubstantial with the Father as to his divinity and consubstantial with us as to his humanity; 'like us in all things but sin.' He was begotten from the Father before all ages as to his divinity and in these last days, for us and for our salvation, was born as to his humanity of the virgin Mary, the bearer of God.
  We confess that one and the same Christ, Lord, and only-begotten Son, is to be acknowledged in two natures without confusion, change, division, or separation. The distinction between natures was never abolished by their union, but rather the character proper to each of the two natures was preserved as they came together in one person and one hypostasis (or substance)."[3]

- The reference to Mary as the "bearer of God" was a title affirmed by the Council of Ephesus in 431. For more on that council, see discussion below.

- The line that says that Jesus possessed "two natures without confusion, change, division, or separation" is a response to both Eutychianism and Nestorianism.

- In contrast to Eutychianism, the Creed explains that Christ possess two natures without confusion or change.

- Against Nestorianism, Chalcedon further teaches that Christ possesses true deity and true humanity without division or separation.

- These four fences of orthodoxy ("without confusion, change, division, or separation") provide guardrails for articulating the mystery of Christ's incarnation without falling into heretical error.

❖ **For Discussion:** Why is it important to affirm both the true deity and true humanity of Jesus Christ? If Jesus were not fully God or fully man, what would that mean for us as sinful people who need to be reconciled to a holy God?

## V. THE OTHER FOUR ECUMENICAL COUNCILS

_____ The Council of Ephesus _____ (**431**)—At this council, the church sought to protect the doctrine of Christ's deity, even in His incarnation. Accordingly, they affirmed that a proper title for Mary is the term *theotokos*, meaning "bearer of God." The purpose behind this title was not to elevate Mary but to safeguard the deity of Christ. In the Incarnation, God the Son took on flesh and became human. When Mary gave birth to Jesus, the baby in the manger was God incarnate.

_____ The Second Council of Constantinople _____ (**553**)—In the East, even after the Council of Chalcedon, there remained a significant number of people who rejected the hypostatic union, insisting instead that Christ possessed a single nature. The advocates of this view were called "monophysites" (*mono* meaning "one" and *physis* meaning "nature"). Emperor Justinian convened a council to address the controversy over this issue. The council affirmed the Council of Chalcedon, but also condemned the writings of three earlier theologians who had been associated with Nestorius. By condemning these earlier theologians, Justinian hoped to improve relations with the monophysites.

_____ The Third Council of Constantinople _____ (**680**)—The primary question answered at this council was whether Christ possessed one will or two wills. In keeping with the church's teaching that Christ possesses two natures, the council affirmed that He likewise possesses two wills (divine and human). The council was careful to clarify that Christ's human will is always in perfect submission to and accordance with His divine will.

_____ The Second Council of Nicaea _____ (**787**)—In the seventh and eighth centuries, a major debate erupted in the East over the veneration of icons (or images) of Jesus and the saints. Some of the emperors were concerned that icons of Jesus, in particular, violated the Second Commandment (Ex. 20:4) and thus constituted idolatry. In 754, a council met in Hieria to condemn icons. But its rulings were overturned in 787 by the Second Council of Nicaea, which affirmed icons as being orthodox. Those who supported the use of icons argued that icons of Jesus do not violate the Second Commandment because Christ is the image of the invisible God (Col. 1:15; Heb. 1:3).

## VI. EVALUATING COUNCILS AND CREEDS

The seven councils listed above are considered "ecumenical" because they included representatives from both the eastern and western halves of the Roman church. As a result, they are accepted in both Eastern Orthodoxy and Roman Catholicism.

Protestant groups have generally held varied opinions about which councils to accept. Many evangelicals, for example, would not accept the Second Council of Nicaea (787). That council, with its approval of the veneration of icons, is particularly troubling for evangelicals, who rightly view such practices as competing with the purity of worship that God requires.

In learning about church councils and historic creeds, it is important to remember a simple principle: God's Word is our authority over church history and church tradition. That means that the decision of a church council is valid only insofar as it accords with what the Word of God teaches.

Like the noble Bereans (Acts 17:11), believers ought to go to the Scriptures to evaluate the teachings and traditions of men. Paul told the Thessalonians to "examine everything carefully; hold fast to that which is good; abstain from every form of evil" (1 Thess. 5:21–22).

We should be grateful for historic councils that affirm clear biblical truths, like the deity of Christ. But we should also remember that the authority for what we believe is not found in the councils of church history, but in the truth of God's Word.

❖ **For Discussion:** Read Mark 7:6–13. What does this passage teach about the priority of Scripture over religious tradition? How does that principle apply to the authority of God's Word in relationship to church councils?

# SCHISMS, SCHOLARS, AND SOLDIERS

### Anselm, Bernard, and the Crusades

**KEY PASSAGE: 2 Timothy 3:13–15**

*"Evil men and impostors will proceed from bad to worse, deceiving and being deceived. You, however, continue in the things you have learned and become convinced of, knowing from whom you have learned them, and that from childhood you have known the sacred writings which are able to give you the wisdom that leads to salvation through faith which is in Christ Jesus."*

| 1033 **Birth of Anselm** | 1090 **Birth of Bernard** | 1109 **Death of Anselm** | 1153 **Death of Bernard** | 1204 **Fourth Crusade** |

| 1054 **East/West Schism** | 1095 **First Crusade** | 1147 **Second Crusade** | 1187 **Third Crusade** |

## I. SETTING THE STAGE: THE EARLY MIDDLE AGES

In the fifth century (400s), things changed dramatically for the western half of the Roman Empire, which was overrun by Germanic tribal groups (like the Vandals, Goths, Huns, and Saxons). By 476, the western Roman Empire had fallen.

Over the subsequent centuries, those tribal groups eventually formed the nations of Europe. But this process of social transformation took a long time.

As a result, there was less theological development and scholarship in the west during the early Middle Ages. From the sixth through tenth centuries, theological scholarship was largely preserved in monasteries.

In the sixth century (500s), the eastern Roman Empire (also called the Byzantine Empire) attempted to regain the territories in the west that had been lost. For example, the military exploits of Emperor Justinian the Great (483–565) were initially successful.

In the seventh century (600s), an unexpected religious movement arose in Arabia under the leadership of Muhammad (570–632). Islamic armies quickly conquered lands in North Africa and the Middle East, which were under Byzantine control. Jerusalem fell in 637. Within a hundred years after Muhammad's death, large portions of the former Roman Empire were under Muslim control.

Despite significant losses to Muslim armies, the Byzantine Empire would survive until Constantinople was finally defeated by the Turks in the fifteenth century.

During the early Middle Ages, the western church sent missionaries to the Germanic tribal groups, and many of them were converted to Christianity. For example, in the 600s, a missionary named Augustine of Canterbury was sent to Britain to evangelize the Angles and Saxons. Some years before this, a powerful tribe known as the Franks had converted to Christianity. These tribal groups gave their allegiance to the bishop of Rome.

The city of Rome was the most important Christian center in the west. Other important centers (Constantinople, Antioch, Alexandria, and Jerusalem) were located in the east. Because no other city in the west rivaled the religious authority of Rome, the prestige and power of the papacy (the bishopric of Rome) was continually elevated.

In the late 700s, a document known as the "Donation of Constantine" surfaced. It was later proven to be a forgery. The document claimed that prior to his death in 337, Emperor Constantine bequeathed the city of Rome to the bishop of Rome. From the eighth to the thirteenth centuries, popes used the "Donation of Constantine" to assert both their religious and political authority over Rome and the surrounding areas.

Militarily, the popes maintained a good relationship with tribal groups like the Franks. This led to the creation of the Holy Roman Empire, when Charlemagne (king of the Franks) was crowned "Emperor of the Romans" by Pope Leo III on Christmas Day 800.

The ninth and tenth centuries were a period of significant corruption for the popes of Rome. The papacy was fought over by rival groups in Rome who recognized it as a position of great political power.

> ❖ **For Discussion:** Look at the key passage at the beginning of this lesson (2 Timothy 3:13–15). Church history provides a record of corrupt leaders going from bad to worse. What antidote did Paul give Timothy to avoid that kind of corruption? Read verses 16–17. Where can we turn to make sure we are walking in a way that honors the Lord?

## II. SCHISM: THE DIVISION BETWEEN EAST AND WEST

As we enter the high Middle Ages (11th–13th centuries), tensions continued to escalate between the eastern and western halves of Roman Christendom. A number of factors contributed to the strained relationship including:

- ► Cultural and Political Differences: Part of the distancing between the East and West was due to political, cultural, and language differences. The eastern church spoke Greek and was part of the Byzantine Empire. The western church spoke Latin and was connected politically with European powers like the Franks.

- ► The Filioque Clause: In 1014, the western church inserted the phrase "and the Son" into the Latin version of the expanded Nicene Creed (dating back to the Council of Constantinople in 381). The edited Latin Creed taught that the Holy Spirit proceeds from the Father and the Son. In Latin, this phrase is filioque. The eastern church balked at the idea that the western church could unilaterally change one of the historic creeds.

- ► Papal Primacy. In the east, the church viewed the Bishops of Rome and Constantinople as equals. However, Pope Leo IX saw the bishop of Rome as having primacy over the bishops of Constantinople, Antioch, Alexandria, and Jerusalem. Leo IX sent a delegation (led by Cardinal Humbert) to Constantinople in 1054. When the Patriarch of Constantinople refused to grant an audience to the delegation, Humbert issued a papal bull excommunicating the Patriarch. In response, the Patriarch excommunicated the papal delegation.

These events culminated in a split between the two halves of Roman Christendom. The eastern church became known as Eastern Orthodoxy; the western church, as Roman Catholicism.

Later events, including the Fourth Crusade in 1204, would deepen the rift between the Greek (eastern) and Latin (western) churches.

> ❖ **For Discussion:** Look up several of the following passages: Acts 2:33; Romans 8:9; Galatians 4:6; Philippians 1:19; 1 Peter 1:11. What do these passages teach about the Holy Spirit's relationship to Christ? How do these verses relate to the *filioque* controversy discussed above?

## III. SKIRMISHES: THE CRUSADES (1095–1291)

Five decades after the East/West Schism, when Muslim armies again threatened the Byzantine Empire, the eastern emperor asked the west for military help.

In response, Pope Urban II called for a crusade. In all, there would be seven major crusades fought over the next two centuries.

For the next two hundred years, "Christian" armies from Europe engaged in what they claimed was "holy war."

- ► Old Testament passages instructing Israel to fight their enemies were reinterpreted for the church. New Testament passages in which military metaphors are used, like Ephesians 6:10–18, were reimagined in literalistic terms. This misguided approach to interpretation twisted the meaning of Scripture for political purposes.

- ► The theory of a "Just War" dates back to Augustine. It argued that military conflict was justifiable when it was authorized by a legitimate authority and when it had a just cause, such as self-defense or defending others against evil. For those who promoted them, the Crusades were justified because they were sanctioned by the pope, and were fought to defend both the Christian pilgrims who travelled to the Holy Land, and the people of the Byzantine Empire who had asked for help.

- ► Sadly, the Crusades included barbaric atrocities that were decidedly unchristian. These atrocities tarnished the reputation of medieval Christendom and created longstanding tensions between western nations and people groups in the Middle East.

For the first time in church history, different orders of "warrior-monks" came on the scene. These include the Knights Templar (who had their headquarters near the Temple Mount in Jerusalem) and the Knights of St. John.

_____The First Crusade_____ (1095–1099) resulted in the conquest of Jerusalem and the establishment of several crusader kingdoms. From a military perspective, the First Crusade was successful.

When one of the crusader kingdoms, Edessa, fell to Muslim armies, a _____Second Crusade_____ (1147–1149) was commissioned. Bernard of Clairvaux (see below) was one of its supporters. The Second Crusade failed to achieve its military objectives.

_____The Third Crusade_____ (1189–1192) was organized in response to the military conquests of Saladin, the sultan of Egypt and Syria who reconquered Jerusalem in 1187. This crusade involved kings like Frederick Barbarossa of the Holy Roman Empire and Richard "the Lion Heart" of England. In spite of the fame of its leaders, this crusade was unable to reconquer Jerusalem.

The situation worsened dramatically in the year 1204. After a series of political twists and turns, the western crusaders sacked the city of Constantinople. Instead of defending the Byzantine Empire (the initial purpose of the Crusades), the soldiers of the _____Fourth Crusade_____ attacked and looted its capital city. In this way, the crusades may have done more to weaken the Byzantine Empire than to preserve it.

In the subsequent decades, several more crusades would be fought, ending in defeat and disaster. By 1291, the crusaders had been pushed out of the Middle East.

❖ **For Discussion:** Read Ephesians 6:10–18. What is the proper interpretation and application of that passage? What would you say to someone who used that passage to justify going on a crusade?

## IV. SCHOLARS: THE RISE OF SCHOLASTICISM

During this period, things began to change in European education. The first European universities were established, as education shifted from monasteries to universities.

> ► The earliest universities in Europe were started in Bologna (1088), Oxford (1096), and Paris (1150). Cambridge was established in 1209.

A new method of learning, called "Scholasticism," began to develop within monastic schools during the time of Charlemagne (748–814). It became the dominant approach to learning in medieval universities.

Scholasticism accompanied the rediscovery in the west of Greek philosophy, and particularly Aristotle.

Two of the most important scholastics were Anselm of Canterbury (1033–1109) and Thomas Aquinas (1225–1274).

> ► One notable contribution made by Anselm was his articulation of the Satisfaction Theory of the atonement. Rather than seeing Jesus' death as a ransom paid to Satan (a view held by some in the early Middle Ages), Anselm taught that Christ's death satisfied the debt that sinners owe to God. The sixteenth-century Protestant Reformers would build on this understanding of the atonement.

> ► Two centuries after Anselm, Thomas Aquinas wrote two important works: Summa Contra Gentiles and Summa Theologica. In these works, Thomas brought Aristotelian philosophy to bear on Christian theology.

> ► Famously, Thomas articulated several classic arguments for the existence of God. These include the Cosmological Argument (namely, that God is the Unmoved Mover or First Cause of the universe) and the Teleological Argument (that God is the Designer behind the order found in nature).

> ► Through his writings, Thomas became one of the most influential thinkers in the history of the western church.

❖ **For Discussion:** Read Isaiah 53:1–12 in light of Anselm's Satisfaction Theory of the atonement of Christ. In this familiar passage, written roughly 700 years before the birth of Jesus, the prophet Isaiah predicts the sufferings of Jesus. What does a passage like this teach us about the atoning work of Christ on the cross? Who was satisfied as a result of Jesus' death?


## V. TESTIMONIES OF GRACE

As we've seen in this lesson, the Middle Ages includes examples of ecclesiastical corruption, biblical misinterpretation, theological confusion, and political turmoil.

In the midst of the chaos, we still find glimpses of the gospel of grace from Christian leaders like Anselm of Canterbury (1033–1109) and Bernard of Clairvaux (1090–1153).

Anselm (discussed above) served as the Archbishop of Canterbury from 1093–1109. Bernard founded a monastery in France in 1115.

The sixteenth-century Reformers did not agree with everything that Anselm and Bernard taught. However, they saw them as allies with regard to salvation by grace through faith alone, based solely on the finished work of Christ. The selected quotes below are encouraging in that regard.

▶ Sinners are saved, not on the basis of their deeds, but because of God's mercy given through Christ.

> **Anselm:** "What, indeed, can be conceived of more merciful than that God the Father should say to a sinner condemned to eternal torments and lacking any means of redeeming himself, 'Take my only-begotten Son and give him on your behalf,' and that the Son himself should say, 'Take me and redeem yourself.' For it is something of this sort that they say when they call us and draw us towards the Christian faith."[1]

> **Anselm:** "Look, O Lord, upon the face of Your Anointed, who became obedient to You even unto death, and let not the scars of His wounds be hidden from Your eyes forever, that You may remember how great a satisfaction for our sins You have received from Him. Would, O Lord, that You would put in the balance the sins by which we have deserved Your wrath, and the sufferings which Your innocent Son endured for us! Truly, O Lord, His sufferings will appear heavier and more worthy, that through them You should pour out Your mercies upon us, than our sins, that through them You should restrain Your compassion in anger."[2]

▶ The immeasurable imperfections of the believer are covered by the infinite perfections of Christ. We are clothed in His righteousness.

> **Anselm:** "Now then, O great Creator of the light, now forgive my faults, for the immeasurable toils' sake of Your beloved Son. Lord, I beseech You, let my impiety be forgiven because of His piety; my obstinacy because of His meekness; my violence because of His gentleness! Now let His humility win back my pride; His patience, my impatience; His kindness, my hardness; His obedience, my disobedience; His calmness, my disquiet; His pleasantness, my bitterness; His sweetness, my anger; His love, my cruelty."[3]

> **Attributed to Anselm:** "[When you stand before God], if He says that you are a sinner; say, 'Lord, I interpose the death of our Lord Jesus Christ between my sins and You.' If He says that you have deserved condemnation; say, 'Lord, I set the death of our Lord Jesus Christ between my evil deserts and You; and His merits I offer for those which I ought to have, but have not.' If He says that He is angry with you; say, 'Lord, I set the death of our Lord Jesus Christ between Your wrath and me.' And when you have completed this, say again, 'Lord, I set the death of our Lord Jesus Christ between You and me.'"[4]

▶ In the eyes of our holy Judge, the sinner's good works are like filthy rags. The sinner's only hope is to cry out for mercy.

> **Bernard:** "What can all our righteousness be before God? Shall it not, according to the prophet, be viewed as a filthy rag: and, if it be strictly judged, shall not all our righteousness turn out to be mere unrighteousness and deficiency? What, then, shall it be concerning sins, when not even our righteousness itself can answer for itself? Wherefore, vehemently exclaiming with the prophet, 'Enter not into judgment with your servant, O Lord,' let us with all humility, flee to mercy; which alone can save our souls."[5]

> **Bernard:** "Nobody will be justified in His sight by works of the law. . . . Conscious of our deficiency, we shall cry to heaven and God will have mercy on us. And on that day we shall know that God has saved us, not by the righteous works that we ourselves have done, but according to His mercy."[6]

▶ The only way sinners can be justified is through faith in Christ. Because they have no merits of their own, His righteousness is imputed to their account.

> **Bernard:** "For the sake of your sins He will die, for the sake of your justification He will rise, in order that you, having been justified through faith, may have peace with God."[7]

**Bernard:** "For what could man, the slave of sin, fast bound by the devil, do of himself to recover that righteousness which he had formerly lost? Therefore he who lacked righteousness had another's imputed to him. . . . It was man who owed the debt, it was man who paid it. For if one, says [the apostle Paul], died for all, then all were dead, so that, as One bore the sins of all, the satisfaction of One is imputed to all."[8]

▶ Salvation is given to those who have Christ's righteousness imputed to them. This righteousness is given as a gift of God's grace, received through faith in Christ, and not on the basis of works.

**Bernard:** [in a prayer to God]: "As for your justice, so great is the fragrance it diffuses that you are called not only just but even justice itself, the justice that makes men righteous. Your power to make men righteous is measured by your generosity in forgiving. Therefore let the man, who through sorrow for sin hungers and thirsts for righteousness, trust in the One who changes the sinner into a righteous man, and judged righteous in terms of faith alone, he will have peace with God."[9]

**Bernard:** "I confess myself most unworthy of the glory of heaven, and that I can never obtain it by my own merits. But my Lord possesses it upon a double title: that of natural inheritance, by being the only begotten Son of his eternal Father; and that of purchase, he having bought it with his precious blood. This second title he has conferred on me; and, upon this right, I hope with an assured confidence, to obtain it through his praiseworthy passion and mercy."[10]

In the centuries after Bernard, we begin to see the rise of _____"pre-Reformers"_____ like Peter Waldo (c. 1140–1205), John Wycliffe (c. 1320–1384), and Jan Hus (c. 1369–1415). These men paved the way for the sixteenth-century Reformers like Luther and Calvin.

❖ **For Discussion:** From the above citations (from Anselm and Bernard), which specific statements stood out to you? Why?

# FORERUNNERS TO THE REFORMATION

Waldo, Wycliffe, and the Pre-Reformers

---

**KEY PASSAGE: Acts 5:29–32**

*"Peter and the apostles answered, 'We must obey God rather than men. The God of our fathers raised up Jesus, whom you had put to death by hanging Him on a cross. He is the one whom God exalted to His right hand as a Prince and a Savior, to grant repentance to Israel, and forgiveness of sins. And we are witnesses of these things; and so is the Holy Spirit, whom God has given to those who obey Him.'"*

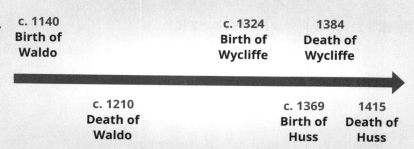

| c. 1140 Birth of Waldo | c. 1324 Birth of Wycliffe | 1384 Death of Wycliffe |

| c. 1210 Death of Waldo | c. 1369 Birth of Huss | 1415 Death of Huss |

---

## I. THE PAPACY IN THE HIGH AND LATE MIDDLE AGES

Papal power reached its zenith under Pope Innocent III (1160–1216). During his tenure, the Fourth Council of the Lateran (1215) dogmatized the doctrine of transubstantiation. This is the erroneous notion that the elements in Communion (the bread and the cup) are physically transformed (in terms of their substance) into the body and blood of Jesus.

Around 1230, the Western church adopted the idea of a Treasure House of Merit in heaven, from which the pope could dispense indulgences (pardons reducing the amount of punishment for sin). The notion of papal indulgences is not biblical, but it dominated the Roman Catholicism of the late Middle Ages.

It did not take long for the system of indulgences to be abused. By offering indulgences in exchange for monetary tithes, the Roman Catholic Church was able to raise significant sums of money. The sale of indulgences became a major fundraising tool for late-medieval popes.

In the 1300s, due to political infighting in Europe, the papacy relocated from Rome to Avignon, France, where it remained for about seventy years. Pope Gregory XI finally returned the papacy to Rome. When his successor, Urban VI, insisted on staying in Rome, French cardinals elected a rival pope (Clement VII) in Avignon.

In 1409, the Council of Pisa attempted to resolve this schism. But this only resulted in the election of a third rival pope. The Papal Schism (also called the Western Schism) was not resolved until the Council of Constance in 1417.

By the late 1400s, the Roman Catholic Church in Europe was in desperate need of a reformation. The corruption of the papacy was evident—from the sale of _____ indulgences _____ to the papal _____ schism, _____ in which _____ three _____ rival popes each claimed to be the true leader of the church.

In the midst of this, God raised up voices of protest who were willing to confront papal corruption and even defy papal authority when it conflicted with the teaching of Scripture.

These courageous individuals are known as "forerunners to the Reformation." Their bold convictions anticipated the stand the Protestant Reformers would take in the sixteenth century.

❖ **For Discussion:** Can you name some biblical figures who took a stand for truth in the face of a corrupt political or religious system? What gave them the courage to take that stand?

## II. PETER WALDO (c. 1140–1210)

Waldo lived from around 1140 to 1210. He was a merchant from Lyon (in modern-day France).

After being influenced by the story of a fourth-century Christian named Alexius (a man who sold all of his belongings in devotion to Christ), Waldo sold his belongings and began a life of preaching and service to the Lord.

Initially, Waldo and his followers were known as the _____"Poor of Lyon."_____ They would later become known as the _____Waldensians._____

Waldo loved the Word of God and commissioned a translation of portions of Scripture from the Latin Vulgate into a local dialect. His reading of Scripture inspired and informed his preaching ministry.

The Roman Catholic Church denounced the Waldensian movement at the Third Lateran Council in 1179. Though he did not receive authorization from the pope, Waldo determined to continue preaching anyway. He boldly insisted that it is better to obey God than men (see Acts 5:29).

Waldo and his followers were subsequently persecuted by Roman Catholic authorities as heretics. However, the movement survived, though the Waldensians were often forced into hiding in the Alps.

The Waldensians shared several important convictions with the later Reformers:

1. _____the authority of Scripture over the authority of the pope_____

2. _____the need to translate Scripture into the common language_____

3. _____the ability of lay people to understand and preach God's Word_____

In the sixteenth century, the Waldensians would join the Reformed branch of the Protestant Reformation. This was fitting, since their movement was a precursor to the Reformation.

❖ **For Discussion:** Look at the key passage at the beginning of this lesson (Acts 5:29–32). When the religious authorities told Peter to stop preaching, what was his response? How did Peter Waldo and his followers apply that same principle to their situation?

## III. JOHN WYCLIFFE (c. 1324–1384)

The Waldensian movement was primarily a movement of the laity (or non-clergy). With John Wycliffe, an English priest and professor at Oxford (Balliol College), we have the beginnings of a scholarly movement of resistance against the corruptions of the papacy.

Accordingly, Wycliffe is known as "the _____Morning Star_____ of the Reformation."

He did not shy away from pointing out the corruption he observed within the priesthood and leadership of the church. His criticism of the papacy was especially pointed.

Wycliffe advocated the translation of the Bible into the common language. Along with some of his colleagues at Oxford, he was involved in translating Scripture from the _____Latin Vulgate_____ into English.

It is likely that Wycliffe translated large portions of the New Testament, including the four Gospels. The rest of the New Testament and the entirety of the Old Testament were translated by his associates.

In his writings, Wycliffe thundered against Roman Catholic abuses. He rejected the doctrine of _____transubstantiation,_____ and disapproved of both _____the sale of indulgences_____ and the mandatory _____celibacy_____ of priests. Furthermore, he insisted that the church should give up its property holdings and that the clergy should embrace a life of poverty and simple devotion to Christ.

Wycliffe also taught that the church was made up of the souls of the elect. This "invisible church" was different from the "visible church" of priests, cardinals, and popes. The distinction between the visible and invisible church would continue to be an important point of emphasis during the Protestant Reformation.

His followers were known as the Lollards. This term seems to mean "mumbler" and was a pejorative term given to this group by their opponents. Like Wycliffe, the Lollards were committed to the authority of Scripture and advocated its translation into the English language.

Wycliffe died of natural causes in 1384. But his views were very influential in England and beyond. Having been declared a heretic (by the Council of Constance in 1415), Wycliffe's body was eventually exhumed (in 1428) and burned in effigy.

Like the Waldensians, Wycliffe and his followers advocated doctrines that would lay the foundation for the later Protestant Reformation. These include (1) a commitment to the authority of Scripture over that of the pope; (2) a desire to see the Word of God translated into the vernacular; and (3) the conviction that Scripture could be understood by those who did not have formal clerical training.

❖ **For Discussion:** Read Psalm 119:105. Why does the psalmist compare the truth of God's Word to a lamp? What happens if the lamp goes out? Look at verses 157–160. How does the psalmist respond to those who oppose the Word of God?

## A. Wycliffe and the Authority of Scripture

One important way John Wycliffe acted as a forerunner to the Protestant Reformation was by affirming the authority of Scripture above any other religious authority. After the Reformation, this Protestant principle would be summarized by the Latin phrase *sola Scriptura* ("Scripture alone").

Consider the following principles affirmed by Wycliffe on the supremacy and necessity of Scripture.

1. Wycliffe insisted that God's Word was a better source of truth than any collection of popes or priests.

   **John Wycliffe:** "[I believe] that a Christian man well understanding it, may gather sufficient knowledge during his pilgrimage upon earth; that all truth is contained in Scripture; that we should admit of no conclusion not approved there; that there is no court beside the court of heaven; that though there were a hundred popes, and all the friars in the world were turned into cardinals, yet should we learn more from the gospel than we should from all that multitude; and that true sons will in no wise go about to infringe the will and testament of their Heavenly Father."[1]

2. Because they are accountable to the Word of God, all people should be exposed to the truth of Scripture.

   **John Wycliffe:** "Holy Scripture is the faultless, most true, most perfect, and most holy law of God, which it is the duty of all men to learn to know, to defend, and to observe, inasmuch as they are bound to serve the Lord in accordance with it."[2]

3. In order to make the Word of God available to laypeople (non-priests), Wycliffe argued that it ought to be translated (from Latin) into the common language of the people.

   **John Wycliffe:** "Believers should ascertain for themselves the matters of their faith by having the Scriptures in a language which they can fully understand. . . . Christ and His apostles evangelized the greater portion of the world, by making known the Scriptures in a language which was familiar to the people."[3]

4. Given the importance of getting God's Word into people's hands and hearts, those who would prevent such a work are guilty of a great crime against their fellow men.

   **John Wycliffe:** "Certainly, it were less cruelty to keep men from bodily meat and drink, and make them to die bodily, than to keep them from hearing the gospel and God's commands, which are life to the soul. What accursed antichrists are these worldly prelates and curates, who curse men for preaching and hearing of holy scriptures."[4]

5. Wycliffe called the pope "antichrist" because the pope stood at the head of a movement which had placed itself above the Word of God, and which suppressed the translation of God's Word into the common language of the people.

   **John Wycliffe:** "As our Lord Jesus Christ ordained by the writing of the four evangelists, to make his gospel surely known, and maintained against heretics, and men out of the faith; so the devil, even Satan, devises by antichrist and his worldly false clerks, to destroy holy writ and Christian men's belief, by [claiming that] the church is of more authority, and more to be believed than any gospel."[5]

6. Wycliffe's efforts to translate the Bible into English were met with charges of heresy. But he remained confident that his actions met with God's approval.

   **John Wycliffe:** "They say it is heresy to speak of the holy scripture in English, and so they would condemn the Holy Ghost who gave it in tongues to the apostles of Christ, to speak the word of God in all languages that were ordained of God under heaven."[6]

7. Wycliffe saw the diminishment of Scripture as a direct attack on the glory of God. In response, he committed his life to the honor of God and His Word.

   **John Wycliffe:** "Let God be my witness, that before everything I have God's glory in my eye, and the good of the Church, which springs out of reverence for Holy Scripture and following the law of Christ."[7]

For Wycliffe, to suppress the people's access to the Word of God was to defy the authority and honor of God Himself.

Wycliffe's emphasis on the authority of God over His church would be embraced and espoused a generation later by the Bohemian preacher Jan Hus (see below).

A century and a half after Wycliffe, William Tyndale (1494–1536) would continue Wycliffe's legacy with regard to Bible translation. Unlike Wycliffe, who translated the Latin Vulgate into English, Tyndale was able to translate from the Hebrew and Greek.

Most English-speaking Christians take it for granted that we have the Word of God in our own language. We can be thankful for faithful Bible translators, like Wycliffe and Tyndale, who labored to make the English Bible a reality.

> ❖ **For Discussion:** Medieval Roman Catholic authorities actively opposed any attempt to make the Word of God available to people in their own language. Read Ezekiel 34:1–12. That passage was written about Old Testament Israel, but the principle it expresses also applies to church history. What does God think about spiritual leadership that fails to feed the flock?

## IV. JAN HUS (c. 1369–1415)

Jan Hus (or "John Huss") lived in modern-day _____Czech Republic._____ He was from a village called "Husinec" which means "Gooseville." The Bohemian word "hus" means "goose."

He was educated at the University of Prague and was highly influenced by the writings of John Wycliffe.

Hus was also known as a gifted preacher. He preached regularly in the Bethlehem Chapel in the city of Prague. By preaching in the Bohemian language, rather than in Latin, Hus exposed his congregation to the Word of God.

> **Jan Hus:** "I humbly accord faith, i.e. trust, to the holy Scriptures, desiring to hold, believe, and assert whatever is contained in them as long as I have breath in me."[8]

Like Wycliffe, Hus preached against the corruption of the clergy and the sale of indulgences. In his book *On the Church* (*De Ecclesia*), Hus insisted that Christ alone, not the pope, is the head of the church. Hus appealed to Christ as the highest authority over popes, councils, and kings.

He explained that, when the word of the pope came into conflict with the Word of Christ, believers were bound to submit to the Scriptures and obey the Lord.

> **Jan Hus:** "If the papal utterances agree with the law of Christ, they are to be obeyed. If they are at variance with it, then Christ's disciples must stand loyally and manfully with Christ against all papal bulls whatsoever and be ready, if necessary, to endure malediction and death. When the pope uses his power in an unscriptural way, to resist him is not a sin, it is a mandate."[9]

Roman Catholic authorities summoned Hus to defend his views at the Council of Constance. He was promised safe passage. But shortly after his arrival (in 1414), he was arrested and imprisoned.

In 1415, Hus was put on trial. When it became clear that he would not be given an opportunity to explain his views, he declared,

> **Jan Hus:** "I appeal to Jesus Christ, the only judge who is almighty and completely just. In his hands I plead my cause, not on the basis of false witnesses and erring councils, but on truth and justice."[10]

On July 6, 1415, he was led outside the city of Constance and burned at the stake. The English phrase, "Your goose is cooked" comes from his execution. According to *Foxe's Book of Martyrs* (or *Acts and Monuments*), Hus told his executioners: "You are now going to burn a goose (Huss signifying goose in the Bohemian language:) but in a century you will have a swan which you can neither roast nor boil."[11]

Though those words may be only legendary, they demonstrate the close connection between Hus and the Protestant Reformation, since Luther's posting of the *95 Theses* (in 1517) came roughly 100 years after the death of Hus.

When the people of Bohemia heard that Hus had been executed, they were outraged. This resulted in several armed conflicts between the followers of Hus (known as Hussites) and Roman Catholic forces.

A century after Hus, Martin Luther was significantly influenced by the life and writings of the Bohemian martyr. The similarities were so striking that Luther was nicknamed "the Saxon Hus."

❖ **For Discussion:** Read Ephesians 1:18–23. What do these verses teach about the place the Lord Jesus occupies in the church? Why do you think Roman Catholic authorities were angry at Hus for asserting that Christ alone is the head of the church?

## V. THE ROAD TO REFORMATION

As we will see in the next lesson, the foundational issue that sparked the Reformation was the issue of authority in the church.

From a Roman Catholic perspective, the pope was regarded as the head of the church, and the church held authority over the Bible and its interpretation.

The forerunners to the Reformation (or "Pre-Reformers") challenged this notion. They viewed Christ alone as the rightful Head of the church. Consequently, His Word was to be revered as the highest authority for the church.

These Pre-Reformers were convinced that the Word of Christ should be accessible to all people, not just the clergy. Consequently, they advocated the translation of the Scriptures into the common languages of Europe. They also preached and taught in the vernacular.

In response, Roman Catholic authorities branded the Pre-Reformers as heretics, and outlawed their translations of Scripture.

But the Word of God could not be suppressed. In the same way that a rediscovery of God's law sparked a reformation in King Josiah's day (2 Chron. 34–35), so the recovery of Scripture in the Middle Ages would soon erupt in widespread revival and reform.

❖ **For Discussion:** Read Acts 6:7, 12:24, and 19:20. What was the power behind the growth of the early church? What do those verses teach us about the power behind revival and reformation?

# PART IV

# THE REFORMATION AND MODERN PERIOD

## 16TH–20TH CENTURIES

# AFTER DARKNESS, LIGHT
### Luther, Calvin, and the Protestant Reformers

**KEY PASSAGE: Hebrews 4:12**

*"For the word of God is living and active and sharper than any two-edged sword, and piercing as far as the division of soul and spirit, of both joints and marrow, and able to judge the thoughts and intentions of the heart."*

| 1505 | 1521 | 1536 | 1546 | 1564 |
|------|------|------|------|------|
| **Luther Enters Monastery** | **Diet of Worms** | **Calvin's Institutes** | **Death of Luther** | **Death of Calvin** |

| 1517 | 1530 | 1541 | 1556 |
|------|------|------|------|
| **The *95 Theses*** | **Diet of Augsburg** | **Calvin Returns to Geneva** | **Knox in Geneva** |

## I. INTRODUCING THE REFORMATION

From the human perspective, the sixteenth-century Protestant Reformation was possible due to several factors.

► Johann Gutenberg's invention of a moveable-type printing press, around 1450, meant that printed materials could be published quickly and in great quantities, rather than having to be copied by hand. Information in books and pamphlets could now be mass produced.

► The authority and reputation of the papacy declined in the fourteenth and fifteenth centuries—due to issues like the Papal Schism (see previous lesson). European monarchs felt greater freedom to defy papal authority.

► The rise of humanism (the study of the humanities) motivated European scholars to study ancient works of literature, including early manuscripts of the Bible. This led to the recovery of biblical Hebrew and Greek.

These factors set the stage for the Protestant Reformation—the sixteenth-century revival and reform movement that dramatically impacted church history.

But the true catalyst behind the Reformation was the power of the Word of God. As Scripture was studied in its original languages and preached in the vernacular, the Holy Spirit used the truth of His Word to open blind eyes and awaken dead hearts.

The Reformers were also committed to translating the Bible into the common languages of Europe. Thanks to the printing press, copies of Scripture were now available to people like never before.

The Reformers themselves recognized _____God's Word_____ as the power behind their movement. Consider the following quotes from Martin Luther (1483–1546):

> **Martin Luther:** "All I have done is put forth, preach and write the Word of God, and apart from this I have done nothing. . . . It is the Word that has done great things. . . . I have done nothing; the Word has done and achieved everything."[1]

**Martin Luther:** "By the Word the earth has been subdued; by the Word the Church has been saved; and by the Word also it shall be reestablished."[2]

**Martin Luther:** "The pope, Luther, Augustine, [or even] an angel from heaven—these should not be masters, judges or arbiters, but only witnesses, disciples, and confessors of Scripture. Nor should any doctrine be taught or heard in the church except the pure Word of God. Otherwise, let the teachers and the hearers be accursed along with their doctrine."[3]

The Reformers' commitment to Scripture flowed from their conviction that Christ alone is the Head of the church. Consequently, His Word is the ultimate authority over the church.

The Reformation principle of *sola Scriptura* ("Scripture alone") is intended to summarize their commitment to the authority and sufficiency of Scripture. God's Word alone is the authority that establishes what to believe and how to live. The city of Geneva was an important center during the sixteenth-century Reformation. Here is how the Reformers explained their commitment to the authority of God's Word.

**The Geneva Confession of 1536:** "We affirm that we desire to follow Scripture alone as the rule of faith and religion."[4]

It should be noted that the Reformers did not dismiss the value of historical councils and creeds or the writings of the church fathers. But they rightly understood that all of those things are subject to the authority of Scripture (see Acts 17:11).

Armed with a commitment to God and His Word, the Reformers boldly proclaimed the Scriptures in the language of the people. Reformation was the inevitable result, as biblical truth confronted the unbiblical traditions of men (Mark 7:6–13).

❖ **For Discussion:** Look at the key passage listed at the beginning of this lesson (Heb. 4:12). What does that verse teach about the power of Scripture? Ephesians 6:17 refers to the Word of God as "the sword of the Spirit." How can we explain the Bible's supernatural power?

## II. A DRAMATIC CONVERSION

In July 1505, a 21-year-old law student was walking through the German countryside. Unexpectedly, he found himself caught in a thunderstorm. Fearing for his life, he cried out for help—not to God, but to his patron saint. "Saint Anne! Spare me and I will become a monk!"

The danger passed. But the pledge Martin Luther made in that moment was a promise he intended to keep. He left behind the study of law (much to his father's dismay), and entered an Augustinian monastery in the city of Erfurt (located in modern Germany).

Though he had escaped the threat of the thunderstorm, he continued to live under the constant threat of God's holy wrath. He felt a heavy weight of guilt pressing down on his conscience, despite his repeated efforts to assuage it.

In keeping with the dominant Roman Catholic thinking of his day, Luther worked tirelessly to try to earn God's favor and pay the punishment for his sins. He performed severe acts of self-ascetism, like sleeping without blankets and fasting for long periods, which permanently damaged his health. He went to confession so often his confessor had to tell him to stop.

Luther's own assessment of this period of his life was this: "If ever a monk got to heaven by monkery, I would have been the monk."[5]

In the midst of this struggle, Luther became fixated with the phrase "the righteousness of God." All Luther could see in that statement was the perfect standard of God's righteousness, and he knew he fell far short of it (Rom. 3:23). For Luther, the righteousness of God stood as a continual reminder of his own condemnation, because he rightly recognized he was not righteous.

Roughly a decade after entering the monastery, Luther's despair finally began to lift. While teaching through the books of Psalms and Romans, and later Galatians, this desperate monk's eyes were opened to the truth of the gospel of grace.

Through his study of Scripture (specifically, Romans 1:16–17), Luther came to see that the righteousness of God revealed in the gospel is not merely the righteous standard of God, but also the righteous provision of God—in which God reckons believers as righteous by clothing them in the perfect righteousness of His Son.

Luther summarized this remarkable discovery with these exuberant words:

> **Martin Luther:** "At last, meditating day and night and by the mercy of God, I gave heed to the context of the words, 'In it the righteousness of God is revealed, as it is written, "He who through faith is righteous shall live."' Then I began to understand that the righteousness of God is that through which the righteous live by a gift of God, namely by faith. ... Here I felt as if I were entirely born again and had entered paradise itself through the gates that had been flung open. An entirely new side of the Scriptures opened itself to me ... and I extolled my sweetest word with a love as great as the loathing with which before I had hated the term 'the righteousness of God.' Thus, that verse in Paul [Rom. 1:17] was for me truly the gate of paradise."[6]

Luther's decade-long struggle was characterized by frustration and despair. Yet, it ended with the good news of the gospel. As a sinner, he could never earn a right standing before God. But through faith, he could be forgiven and clothed in Christ's righteousness.

Luther would later identify this as the great exchange of the gospel. The penalty for the believer's sin was imputed (or reckoned) to Christ who paid that penalty on the cross. At the same time, the perfect righteousness of Christ is imputed to the believer, who is declared righteous by God (2 Cor. 5:21).

No message is more important than the good news of God's grace. No sinner is good enough to earn God's favor. All of us stand in desperate need of divine mercy.

The drama surrounding Luther's conversion may be unique to him, but the recognition of personal unworthiness and the need for God's grace is something every true believer has experienced firsthand.

When we reflect on the story of Luther's conversion, along with the larger Reformation that followed it, we simultaneously celebrate the wonder of our own testimony: that we have been saved by grace, not by works, so that no one can boast (Eph. 2:8–9).

❖ **For Discussion:** Every testimony of God's grace is amazing. Take a moment to reflect on the events that led to your conversion. Share a brief testimony of God's grace in your life with others in your class or discussion group.

## III. *95 THESES* & THE DIET OF WORMS

In the previous lesson, we introduced "indulgences" (pardons that supposedly reduced the punishment for sin). The medieval church issued indulgences in exchange for money (tithes). This selling of indulgences became an important source of income for the papacy.

In 1517, church authorities commissioned a monk named _____Johann Tetzel_____ to sell indulgences throughout Saxony.

By this time, Luther was teaching at the University of Wittenberg. When Tetzel began selling indulgences near Wittenberg, Luther was incensed.

To articulate his concerns, Luther drafted a list of 95 arguments against the abuse of indulgences. This treatise was written in Latin, and was intended for inter-church debate.

Somehow, Luther's Latin document was translated into German. The printing press made it possible for copies to be quickly distributed throughout Saxony and the surrounding regions. Luther had given voice to popular concerns about corruption in the church.

In spite of the growing outcry, Roman Catholic authorities were slow to respond. Initially, the pope hoped it would be handled within the Augustinian monastic order, of which Luther was a part.

In July 1519, Luther debated a man named Johann Eck on the topic of papal authority. Luther admitted that he admired the teachings of Jan Hus, which was a dangerous thing to do, since Hus had been executed as a heretic.

In June 1520, Pope Leo X issued a decree (called a papal bull) that threatened to excommunicate Luther if he did not recant. When Luther refused to relinquish his views, he was excommunicated in January 1521.

He was subsequently summoned by Emperor Charles V to an Imperial Council (called a Diet) in the city of Worms. Luther arrived in April and was presented with a list of his alleged heresies. But Luther still refused to recant.

> **Martin Luther:** "Since then your Majesty and your lordships desire a simple reply, I will answer without horns and without teeth. Unless I am convinced by Scripture and plain reason—I do not accept the authority of popes and councils, for they have contradicted each other—my conscience is captive to the Word of God. I cannot and I will not recant anything, for to go against conscience is neither right nor safe. God help me. Amen."[7]

The following month, in May 1521, Luther was declared a "notorious heretic" by the emperor. This designation made him an outlaw and put his life in danger.

Luther's political protector was a prince in the Holy Roman Empire named Frederick III, also known as Frederick "the Wise" of Saxony. Knowing Luther was in imminent danger, Frederick sent men to "kidnap" Luther and take him into hiding.

Using the pseudonym "Junker Jorge" (Squire George), Luther spent most of the next year in the Wartburg Castle. While there, he translated the New Testament from Greek into the German language. This translation was completed early in 1522.

Luther's German translation would be influential on the translation efforts of William Tyndale, who was translating the New Testament into English—a task he completed in 1525.

This time in Luther's life illustrates his commitment to the authority of Scripture. He refused to waver in his commitment to biblical truth, even when threatened by the pope and the emperor. That same conviction motivated his translation efforts, because he recognized the need to make the Scripture available to the common people.

> ❖ **For Discussion:** Look at what Luther said at the Diet of Worms. To what authority did Luther appeal? To what authority was his conscience bound?

## IV. THE HEART OF THE GOSPEL

In keeping with their commitment to the _____authority_____ of Scripture, Luther and his fellow Reformers looked to God's Word to define the heart of the gospel.

During the Middle Ages, the doctrine of justification had become confused and distorted. Roman Catholics saw justification as a gradual process, by which the sinner was made righteous over a long period of time. This process involved both God's grace and the sinner's efforts to perform good works.

Part of the confusion about justification was due to the Latin translation of the Greek term. The Latin term (*iustificare*) could mean "to make righteous" and lent itself toward a process. But the Greek term (*dikaiosuné*) means "to declare righteous," which speaks of a judicial verdict issued at a moment in time.

With the rediscovery of biblical Greek, the Reformers were careful to correct the erroneous notion that justification was a process procured in part by good works. Rather, it is a divine pardon issued at the moment of conversion, in which God declares the sinner to be righteous (or justified) based on the atoning work and imputed righteousness of Christ.

Thus, the Reformers taught that believers are saved by grace alone (*sola gratia*) through faith alone (*sola fide*) in the person and work of Christ alone (*solus Christus*). All of the glory for their salvation goes to God alone (*soli Deo Gloria*). They recognized the vital importance of repentance but clearly saw good works as the *evidence* or *fruit* of justification, not the *cause* or *root* of it.

Luther distinguished the biblical gospel from Roman Catholic teaching by differentiating between the "theology of the cross" (the biblical view) and the "theology of glory" (the Roman view).

► The "theology of the cross" emphasized that human beings can do nothing to earn their own righteousness before God; nor can they add anything to the righteousness provided for them through Christ. Any righteousness given to them comes from outside of them (it is an "alien righteousness").

► On the other hand, the "theology of glory" (as Luther called it), taught that, even after the fall, there remained some ability in sinful people to achieve their own righteousness before God. This view implied that part of the credit or glory for salvation belongs to the sinner. Luther and his fellow Reformers rejected this and rightly insisted that all the glory for salvation belongs to God alone.

Below are some representative statements from Martin Luther and John Calvin (1509–1564) on the doctrine of justification by grace through faith alone.

**Martin Luther:** "Through faith in Christ, therefore, Christ's righteousness becomes our righteousness and all that he has becomes ours; rather, he himself becomes ours. . . . This is an infinite righteousness, and one that swallows up all sin in a moment, for it is impossible that sin should exist in Christ. On the contrary, he who trusts in Christ exists in Christ; he is one with Christ, having the same righteousness as he."[8]

**Martin Luther:** "So making a happy change with us, He [Christ] took upon Him our sinful person and gave unto us His innocent and victorious person; wherewith we being now clothed, are freed from the curse of the law. . . . By faith alone therefore we are made righteousness, for faith lays hold of this innocence and victory of Christ."[9]

**John Calvin:** "Justified by faith is he who, excluded from the righteousness of works, grasps the righteousness of Christ through faith, and clothed in it, appears in God's sight not as a sinner but as a righteous man."[10]

**John Calvin:** "We are justified before God solely by the intercession of Christ's righteousness. This is equivalent to saying that man is not righteous in himself but because the righteousness of Christ is communicated to him by imputation."[11]

In defending their understanding of the gospel, the Reformers returned to the teaching of Scripture. Some of the key passages to which they looked include:

> Luke 18:10–14; 23:43
> John 3:16, 36; 11:25–27
> Acts 13:38–39; 15:9–11; 16:30–31
> Romans 3:28; 4:3; 5:1–3; 11:6
> 2 Corinthians 5:21
> Galatians 1:6–9; 2:21
> Colossians 2:13–14
> Ephesians 2:4–10
> Philippians 3:7–11
> 1 Timothy 1:15–17
> Titus 3:4–7

❖ **For Discussion:** Look up two or three of the Scripture passages listed above. What do those passages teach about the grace of the gospel? What would you say to someone who thinks that they can get to heaven on the basis of their own good works?

## V. JOHN CALVIN AND THE GLORY OF GOD

Calvin was born in France in 1509. He was twenty-five years younger than Luther. As such, Calvin represents the _____second generation_____ of Protestant Reformers.

Calvin was converted in the early 1530s. Like Luther, he had been studying to be a lawyer before God changed the course of his life. When persecution against Protestants erupted in France, Calvin fled to Switzerland.

In Basel, he penned his first edition of the *Institutes of the Christian Religion*. It was published in 1536.

Later that same year, he was planning to travel to Strasbourg. His journey took him through Geneva, where another Reformer named William Farel (1489–1565) convinced him to stay and help lead the Protestant church in Geneva.

In 1538, Farel and Calvin came into conflict with the city council and were forced to leave Geneva. Calvin travelled to Strasbourg, where he got married and published his first commentary on the book of Romans and his second edition of the *Institutes*.

In the summer of 1541, Calvin returned to Geneva. He would minister there for the rest of his life. During his time in Geneva, he preached over 2,000 sermons.

By 1546, Calvin began to face opposition from some of the citizens of Geneva. This opposition group (known as the Libertines) resisted Calvin and the rules that were enacted by the church in Geneva. It was not until nearly ten years later, in the mid 1550s, that the opposition against Calvin finally began to wane.

Beginning in 1555, Calvin welcomed English Protestant refugees (who were fleeing from the Roman Catholic Queen Mary I) to Geneva. Among them was the Scottish preacher John Knox.

In 1558, Calvin became ill and worked quickly to finish up the final edition of his *Institutes*. This final version (published in 1559) expanded to 80 chapters, from the original six chapters in the first edition.

Calvin died on May 27, 1564. The aim of his life had been the glory of God. Though his legacy is often reduced to a few key points related to God's sovereignty in salvation, Calvin's ministry focused on the sovereign glory of God in everything.

> **John Calvin:** "The Holy Spirit has consecrated us as temples of God. We, therefore, must let the glory of God shine through us, and we must not pollute ourselves with sin."[12]

> **John Calvin:** "For what is more consonant with faith than to recognize that we are naked of all virtue, in order to be clothed by God? That we are empty of all good, to be filled by him? That we are slaves of sin, to be freed by him? Blind, to be illumined by him? Lame, to be made straight by him? Weak, to be sustained by him? To take away from us all occasion for glorying, that he alone may stand forth gloriously and we glory in him?"[13]

> **John Calvin:** "For until men recognize that they owe everything to God, that they are nourished by his fatherly care, that he is the Author of their every good, that they should seek nothing beyond him—they will never yield him willing service. Nay, unless they establish their complete happiness in him, they will never give themselves truly and sincerely to him."[14]

❖ **For Discussion:** Read 1 Corinthians 10:31. What does it mean to do all things for God's glory? How should that priority impact the way we live as believers (2 Cor. 5:9)?

## VI. OTHER PEOPLE YOU SHOULD KNOW

**Philip Melanchthon (1497–1560)**—Close associate of Luther in Wittenberg. He was the principal author of the Augsburg Confession, which was presented to Emperor Charles V at the Diet of _____Augsburg_____ in 1530. The Augsburg Confession is one of the most important documents in Lutheran history.

**Ulrich Zwingli (1484–1531)**—Protestant Reformer in Zurich, who is considered the father of the Reformed branch of the Reformation. He convinced the Zurich city council to allow him to make sweeping ecclesiastical reforms, including the abolishment of the mass. A contemporary of Luther, the two agreed on many doctrinal issues but differed sharply on their understanding of the Lord's Table.

**William Tyndale (1494–1536)**—English Bible translator who fled to Europe because translating was illegal in England at the time. He translated the New Testament from Greek and the Pentateuch from Hebrew. In 1536, he was arrested and executed by command of Henry VIII, the King of England. His translation efforts laid the groundwork for subsequent English Bible translations.

**Thomas Cranmer (1489–1556)**—Protestant Archbishop of _____Canterbury_____ who helped spark the Reformation in England during the reigns of Henry VIII and Edward VI. Cranmer was executed for his faith by Mary I (known as "Bloody Mary").

**John Knox (c. 1513–1572)**—Scottish Reformer who was exiled to England, and then to Europe (Frankfurt and Geneva) before returning to Scotland to lead the Reformation efforts there. He came into conflict with the Roman Catholic ruler Mary Queen of Scots. In the end, Knox brought Reformed theology to Scotland, thereby founding Presbyterianism.

**KEY PASSAGE: John 3:1–3**

*"Now there was a man of the Pharisees, named Nicodemus, a ruler of the Jews; this man came to Jesus by night and said to Him, 'Rabbi, we know that You have come from God as a teacher; for no one can do these signs that You do unless God is with him.' Jesus answered and said to him, 'Truly, truly, I say to you, unless one is born again he cannot see the kingdom of God.'"*

| 1620 Pilgrims to Plymouth | 1640s English Civil War | 1660 Restoration | 1703 Births of Edwards and Wesley | 1739–41 Great Awakening |
| --- | --- | --- | --- | --- |
| 1630s–40s Puritans to New England | 1650s Cromwell's Protectorate | 1662–1684 Puritans as Non-Conformists | | 1730s–40s Evangelical Revival |

## I. THE ENGLISH PURITANS

During the reign of Mary I, known as "Bloody Mary" (from 1553–1558), English Protestants were severely persecuted. Many fled from England to cities like Geneva and Frankfurt.

When they returned home to England, after Queen Elizabeth I was crowned in 1558, they wanted to see the Church of England implement the same reforms they had observed in the Protestant congregations of Europe.

These English Protestants sought to purify the church of any remaining Roman Catholic corruption. For this reason, they became known as "Puritans."

Under Elizabeth (1558–1603), English Protestantism (or Anglicanism) retained elements of Roman Catholic liturgy. This proved frustrating to the Puritans.

When James VI of Scotland became James I of England (in 1603), the Puritans hoped he would be more friendly to their intended reforms. But in 1604, at the Hampton Court Conference, James made it clear he did not intend to support the Puritan cause. However, he did commission a new English translation of the Bible. The King James version would be completed in 1611.

Under James I, Puritans continued to be frustrated.

The situation worsened in 1625, when Charles I came to the throne. Charles had married a Roman Catholic queen. He also appointed William Laud (1573–1645) as the Archbishop of Canterbury.

> Laud opposed the Puritans, persecuting Puritan pastors who deviated from Anglican liturgy prescribed in *The Book of Common Prayer* and prohibiting them from teaching on God's sovereignty in salvation.

These conflicts eventually reached a breaking point, leading to the English Civil War (from 1641–1651), during which the Puritan supporters of Parliament fought against the Royalist supporters of Charles I.

> Parliament won the war. Charles was executed in 1649, and his family was exiled to the Netherlands.

> A Puritan general named Oliver Cromwell (1599–1658) came to power during the Protectorate (1653–1659).

During the war, Puritan theologians met at the Westminster Assembly (from 1643–1653) and drafted the Westminster Confession and Catechisms. From 1645–1660, the Westminster Standards were adopted in the English church.

The Puritans were finally able to implement their desired changes to the Church of England.

After Cromwell's death, Charles II returned from the Netherlands and was crowned king (in 1660). When the monarchy was restored in England, the Church of England returned to its status prior to the English Civil War.

As a result, roughly 2,400 Puritan pastors were forced out of the church in 1662 (in what is known as the "Great Ejection"). These Puritans became known as "dissenters" and "nonconformists."

The dissenters formed their own separate congregations, and faced legal consequences as a result. For example, John Bunyan (1628–1688), the author of *Pilgrim's Progress*, was imprisoned for twelve years for preaching without a license.

With the Puritans sidelined, England entered a period of deep spiritual decline at the end of the seventeenth century. At the dawn of the eighteenth century, the need for revival was great.

❖ **For Discussion:** The Puritans were the theologically conservative, Bible-believing Christians in England in the sixteenth and seventeenth centuries. Their desire was to purify the Church of England by ridding it of unbiblical doctrines and practices. What lessons can contemporary Christians learn from the example of the Puritans?

## II. PURITANISM AND AMERICA

The Pilgrims were a group of separatist Puritans who left England due to religious _____persecution_____ (during the reign of James I). After spending a short time in Amsterdam, they embarked for North America on the *Mayflower*, landing at Plymouth in 1620.

After Charles I came to the throne, many more Puritans left England, convinced that the persecution in their homeland would only grow worse. The "Great Migration" of the 1630s saw some 20,000 settlers (mostly Puritans) emigrate to New England.

▶ The Plymouth Colony was established in 1620, and the Massachusetts Bay Colony in 1628.

▶ In 1636, Harvard University was founded.

▶ Around that same time, Roger Williams left Massachusetts Bay to establish Rhode Island, and the first Baptist Church in America (in 1638).

The initial wave of Puritans in New England was very devout. But subsequent generations lacked the conviction of their predecessors. Over time, a growing sense of spiritual indifference set in.

By the time of Jonathan Edwards (1703–1758), the churches of New England were largely populated by nominal Christians.

In both England and New England, there was a great need for revival; such paved the way for the ministries and impact of men like Jonathan Edwards and George Whitefield.

❖ **For Discussion:** In Judges 2:6–15, the author describes what happened to Israel when later generations did not follow the Lord like their forefathers had done. As noted above, subsequent generations of American Puritans lacked the fervent love for the Lord that had characterized their ancestors. What factors do you think contribute to that kind of apathy? How should that affect the way we think about the next generation in the church?

## III. THE EVANGELICAL REVIVAL IN ENGLAND

Due to spiritual decline in both England and the American colonies, the stage was set for an Evangelical Revival in England and a Great Awakening in America.

To that end, God raised up key leaders, including Jonathan Edwards (1703–1758), John Wesley (1703–1791), Charles Wesley (1707–1788), and George Whitefield (1714–1770).

John and Charles Wesley were born into a large family of nineteen children. Their father was an Anglican minister.

George Whitefield, by contrast, was only two years old when his father died. Whitefield grew up in poverty.

In 1729, Charles Wesley founded a group at Oxford University called the "Holy Club." Both his brother, John, and his friend, George Whitefield, would eventually join this group. All three men would later admit they were not converted at this time.

The members of the Holy Club focused on trying to be holy, at least on the outside.

▶ In his efforts to earn salvation through external good works, George Whitefield forced himself to endure severe discipline which damaged his health. Yet, nothing he did could regenerate his heart or secure his salvation.

Other students at Oxford called the members of the Holy Club "methodists" because of their methodical approach to self-discipline and spirituality. This nickname later came to define the movement these men would lead.

Because Whitefield's family was very poor, when he enrolled at Pembroke College, Oxford, he paid his expenses by working as a "servitor" (an errand boy serving other students).

In 1733, Charles Wesley gave Whitefield a copy of a Puritan work called *The Life of God in the Soul of Man* by Henry Scougal. It showed Whitefield that unless he was born again, he would be condemned by God. The Lord used that book to draw Whitefield to saving faith.

After being genuinely converted, Whitefield embarked on a ministry of evangelism and preaching. When it became difficult to find preaching opportunities in churches, he began to preach outdoors. This would become a hallmark of the Methodist movement.

In 1738, the Lord opened the eyes of both John and Charles Wesley (on different occasions) to the truth of the gospel. Their hearts were transformed. The dead moralism that had previously characterized them was replaced by the true life of regeneration.

That same year, Whitefield made his first voyage to the American colonies. His first visit was to the colony of Georgia. A couple years later, he would tour New England, preaching in major cities like New York and Boston. This preaching tour corresponds with a revival in America known as the Great Awakening (see below).

After returning to England in the 1740s, Whitefield encountered resistance from John Wesley over the doctrine of God's sovereignty in salvation. This resulted in early Methodism being split—with Whitefield embracing the Reformed doctrine of election and Wesley advocating an Arminian view that emphasized human free will.

During this time, both John Wesley and George Whitefield significantly influenced people throughout England, calling them to consider whether they had truly been born again. By being willing to preach outside, they were not constrained by the size of local churches or the approval of the clergy.

Whitefield also had a major impact on the American colonies. During his life, he made thirteen trans-Atlantic voyages (for a total of seven trips to America). On his seventh trip, in 1770, he died after preaching in New Hampshire.

> ► Over his life, Whitefield preached some 18,000 sermons. He was the most well-known preacher in both England and New England in the eighteenth century; and one of the most recognizable figures of his day.

In 1788, Charles Wesley died. He is most well-known for composing more than 6,000 hymns, including well-known songs like *And Can It Be* and *O for a Thousand Tongues to Sing*.

John Wesley died in 1791, after giving shape to the Methodist movement. Though he traveled to America only one time, the Methodist movement would become the largest Protestant denomination in America in the nineteenth century.

> ❖ **For Discussion:** The preachers of the Evangelical Revival noted that moral behavior and good works cannot save sinners. Rather, people must be "regenerated" or "born again," meaning that their hearts must be changed. Read John 3:1–3, 2 Corinthians 5:17, and Titus 3:1–7. What do these passages teach about the relationship between regeneration and salvation?

## IV. JONATHAN EDWARDS AND THE GREAT AWAKENING

### A. Edwards's Early Life

Edwards was born on October 5, 1703. He was the fifth of eleven children and the only boy. His father, Timothy Edwards, was a minister, as was his maternal grandfather, _____Solomon Stoddard._____

As a young teenager, Edwards started college at Yale. During his time there, at age 16, he became very ill and thought he was going to die. This resulted in a period of sober reflection, during which he considered the condition of his soul.

In 1721, he embraced the Lord Jesus in saving faith. As a result of his conversion, he came to love the doctrine of God's sovereignty, a doctrine he had struggled to embrace earlier.

Over the next few years, Edwards penned _____seventy_____ resolutions in which he articulated his desire to glorify God and walk in loving obedience to Him. Here are several excerpts from his *Resolutions*:

> **Jonathan Edwards (Preface):** "Being sensible that I am unable to do anything without God's help, I do humbly entreat him by his grace to enable me to keep these Resolutions, so far as they are agreeable to his will, for Christ's sake."

> 4. "Resolved, never to do any manner of thing, whether in soul or body, less or more, but what tends

to the glory of God; nor be, nor suffer it, if I can avoid it."

5. "Resolved, never to lose one moment of time; but improve it the most profitable way I possibly can."

16. "Resolved, never to speak evil of anyone, so that it shall tend to his dishonor, more or less, upon no account except for some real good."

21. "Resolved, never to do anything, which if I should see in another, I should count a just occasion to despise him for, or to think any way the more meanly of him."

48. "Resolved, constantly, with the utmost niceness and diligence, and the strictest scrutiny, to be looking into the state of my soul, that I may know whether I have truly an interest in Christ or no; that when I come to die, I may not have any negligence respecting this to repent of."

52. "I frequently hear persons in old age say how they would live, if they were to live their lives over again: Resolved, that I will live just so as I can think I shall wish I had done, supposing I live to old age."[1]

In the midst of writing his resolutions, Edwards ministered briefly at a church in New York (in 1722–1723) and later served as a tutor at Yale College (1724–1726).

In 1727, Edwards was ordained in Northampton, Massachusetts, where he would assist his grandfather (Solomon Stoddard) in pastoral ministry. A couple years later, when Stoddard died, Edwards became the pastor of the church.

In 1727, he married Sarah Pierpont. Together, they had eleven children.

## B. The Great Awakening

In the mid to late 1730s, Edwards's church became the starting point for a _____revival_____ that spread throughout the surrounding areas.

In 1740, George Whitefield came to Northampton to preach, as part of his preaching tour through New England. The Lord used Whitefield's evangelistic preaching to convict the hearts of many who had grown up in the church but had never been truly converted to Christ.

Many throughout New England were awakened to the deadness of their hypocritical religion and came to saving faith. This movement is known as the Great Awakening.

In 1741, Edwards preached his famous sermon, *Sinners in the Hands of an Angry God,* to a congregation in Enfield, Connecticut. The sermon stirred up many in the congregation to cry out for God's mercy and repent of their hypocrisy.

In the 1740s, in response to the dramatic conversions that occurred during the Great Awakening, Edwards emphasized the fruit of genuine salvation. Works like *A Treatise on Religious Affections* (published in 1746) explained that true conversion is evidenced by spiritual fruit, like love for God and others.

## C. Edwards's Later Life

In 1747, Edwards was impacted by the life and death of David Brainerd, who served as a missionary to Native American tribes in New England. In 1749, Edwards published Brainerd's biography and diary. This work would influence later missionaries, such as William Carey (see next lesson).

Due to a number of issues, including his refusal to serve communion to church members who had not been truly converted, Edwards was voted out of his church after serving there for more than twenty years. He preached his *Farewell Sermon* in 1750.

Edwards moved to Stockbridge, Massachusetts, where he followed in the footsteps of Brainerd, engaging in evangelistic outreach to a local Native American tribe.

During this time, he also published a treatise on the *Freedom of the Will*. This important work demonstrated the compatibilism between God's sovereignty and man's will.

In 1758, Edwards moved to New Jersey to serve as the president of the College of New Jersey (later called Princeton University). Shortly after he arrived, he was inoculated for smallpox. Instead of preserving his health, the inoculation proved fatal. Edwards died on March 22, 1758.

Even though he was only fifty-four years old when he died, he remains one of America's most influential theologians.

> ❖ **For Discussion:** The Great Awakening was a revival among the churches of New England. People who had grown up in church but had never embraced Christ in saving faith were suddenly confronted with the reality of their spiritual condition. What would you say to someone who claims to be a Christian simply because they attend church and try to be a good person? What passages of Scripture would you use to explain what it truly means to follow Christ?

## V. IN THE FOOTSTEPS OF THE REFORMATION

At its core, the Protestant Reformation was built on two foundational principles. ____"Scripture alone"____ (*sola Scriptura*) provided the authority for defining doctrine and determining convictions. ____"Faith alone"____ (*sola fide*) articulated the truth of the gospel, that sinners are justified (or declared righteous in God's sight) by grace through faith in Jesus Christ, apart from their own self-righteous works.

These two principles are clearly evidenced by both the Puritans and the eighteenth-century church leaders who followed them. Consider the Westminster Confession regarding both the authority of Scripture and justification by faith:

*The Westminster Confession* on Scripture: "The authority of the Holy Scripture, for which it ought to be believed, and obeyed, dependeth not upon the testimony of any man, or church; but wholly upon God (who is truth itself) the author thereof: and therefore it is to be received, because it is the Word of God. . . . The supreme judge by which all controversies of religion are to be determined, and all decrees of councils, opinions of ancient writers, doctrines of men, and private spirits, are to be examined, and in whose sentence we are to rest, can be no other but the Holy Spirit speaking in the Scripture." (1.4, 10)

*The Westminster Confession* on justification: "Those whom God effectually calleth, he also freely justifieth: not by infusing righteousness into them, but by pardoning their sins and by accounting and accepting their persons as righteous; not for anything wrought in them, or done by them, but for Christ's sake alone; nor by imputing faith itself, the act of believing, or any other evangelical obedience to them, as their righteousness; but by imputing the obedience and satisfaction of Christ unto them, they receiving and resting on him and his righteousness, by faith; which faith they have not of themselves, it is the gift of God." (11.1)

The Protestant evangelists of the eighteenth century—like Edwards, Whitefield, and the Wesleys—would have agreed that God's Word comes with His supreme authority, and that God's work of salvation is based solely on the finished work of Christ, not the self-righteous efforts of the sinner.

❖ **For Discussion:** This lesson focused on the effects of the Reformation in the seventeenth and eighteenth centuries. What stood out most to you about either the Puritans or the preachers of the Evangelical Revival and Great Awakening?

# Lesson 12

# THE GOSPEL GOES FORTH

Carey, Judson, and the Modern Missions Movement

**KEY PASSAGE: Matthew 28:18–20**

*"Jesus came up and spoke to them, saying, 'All authority has been given to Me in heaven and on earth. Go therefore and make disciples of all the nations, baptizing them in the name of the Father and the Son and the Holy Spirit, teaching them to observe all that I commanded you; and lo, I am with you always, even to the end of the age.'"*

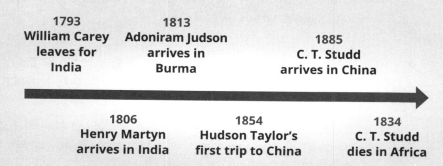

**1793** William Carey leaves for India

**1813** Adoniram Judson arrives in Burma

**1885** C. T. Studd arrives in China

**1806** Henry Martyn arrives in India

**1854** Hudson Taylor's first trip to China

**1834** C. T. Studd dies in Africa

## I. THE GREAT COMMISSION & MODERN MISSIONS

After His resurrection, the Lord Jesus commissioned His followers to be His witnesses throughout the world (Matt. 28:18–20; Acts 1:8).

In the sixteenth century, the Protestant Reformers courageously committed themselves to translating the Bible and preaching its truth. That same priority characterized the missionary movement of the nineteenth and twentieth centuries.

Consider the following examples of faithful believers who took Christ's mandate seriously, to go and make disciples of all nations.

1. _____John Elliott_____ (1604–1690) was a Puritan settler in New England who began evangelizing the Native Americans. Known as the "apostle to the Indians," he translated the Bible into their native language, helped to establish churches, and sparked a missionary zeal among Christian settlers in the New World.

2. That missionary spirit inspired men like _____David Brainerd_____ (1718–1747) to similarly devote his life to reaching Native Americans with the good news of the gospel.

3. Though Brainerd died at only 29 years of age, his friend _____Jonathan Edwards_____ (1703–1758) was so impressed by the young missionary's passion that he edited Brainerd's diary and published it. Edwards himself would later work as a missionary to the Native Americans of Stockbridge, Massachusetts.

4. In 1785, an English shoe cobbler named _____William Carey_____ (1761–1834) read a copy of *An Account of the Life of the Late Rev. David Brainerd* by Jonathan Edwards. The book had a profound impact on Carey's thinking, igniting a passion in his heart to take the gospel to India. William Carey left for India in 1793 and the modern missions movement was born.

5. Carey's example influenced American missionary _____Adoniram Judson_____ (1788–1850). It inspired others also. In 1802, a British preacher named _____Charles Simeon_____ (1759–1836) was speaking about the good that William Carey was doing in India. Upon hearing that message, a young man in the

congregation named _____Henry Martyn_____ (1781–1812) determined that he, too, would go to India, rather than going to law school.

6. Martyn died young. Yet his memoirs influenced many in England. In particular, his biography had a significant impact on ___Anthony Norris Groves___ (1795–1853), who is considered by some to be the "father of faith missions." (Groves was a missionary to modern-day Iraq and later to India). In his own memoirs, Groves writes,

> **Anthony Norris Groves:** "I have today finished reading, for the second time, [Henry] Martyn's Memoir. . . . How my soul admires and loves his zeal, self-denial and devotion; how brilliant, how transient his career; what spiritual and mental power amidst bodily weakness and disease! O, may I be encouraged by his example to press on to a higher mark."[1]

7. In 1825, Groves published a short booklet entitled *Christian Devotedness*, in which he encouraged Christians to live frugally, trust God for their needs, and devote the bulk of their income to evangelism efforts around the world. That book had a major impact on the thinking of men like _____George Müller_____ (1805–1898) and ___James Hudson Taylor___ (1832–1905), significantly shaping the way they thought about missions.

8. Hudson Taylor was the first modern missionary to reach the interior of China. He established the China Inland Mission and recruited hundreds of missionaries to join in evangelistic efforts there. At one point, Taylor returned to England where he urged Christian young people to join him in China. A famous Cambridge cricket player named _____C. T. Studd_____ (1860–1931) was among those profoundly affected by Taylor's preaching. Studd left behind a life of leisure to serve Christ overseas. Six other students joined Studd and together they became known as "The Cambridge Seven."

9. The publicity garnered by C. T. Studd and "The Cambridge Seven" in England, especially in British universities, influenced the beginnings of the Student Volunteer Movement for Foreign Missions (started in 1886) in North America. Under the leadership of men like _____D. L. Moody_____ (1837–1899) and _____Arthur T. Pierson_____ (1837–1911), the author of George Müller's biography, hundreds of American students would join the volunteer movement and commit themselves to foreign missionary work.

10. The testimony of Hudson Taylor was also particularly influential in the lives of later missionaries like _____Amy Carmichael_____ (1867–1951), _____Eric Liddell_____ (1902–1945), and _____Jim Elliot_____ (1927–1956). Speaking of that impact, Elisabeth Elliot explained:

> **Elisabeth Elliot:** "When I was a college student my father lent me the two-volume life of Hudson Taylor. Another college student, Jim Elliot, read it too and this was one of the great things he and I had in common—a huge hunger for that sort of godliness, for a true missionary heart."[2]

As this brief history demonstrates, missions is contagious. From John Elliott to Jim Elliot, a perceptible chain of influence and gospel faithfulness can be traced from one fervent missionary to the next.

Interestingly, this particular chain brings us full circle—from the Americas around the globe and back again. John Elliott took the gospel to the Native Americans of New England. Three centuries later, Jim Elliot took the gospel to the Native Americans of Ecuador.

Some of the missionaries listed above only lived a short time. David Brainerd was twenty-nine years old when he died. Henry Martyn was thirty-one. Jim Elliot was twenty-eight. Yet, the impact of their lives extends far beyond their short tenures on this earth. Their self-sacrifice inspired thousands of others to give their lives for the sake of the gospel.

This is but one small thread in the great tapestry that God has woven throughout the centuries. Yet, it illustrates a profound lesson in a vivid way. Never underestimate the power for influence of a life fully invested in serving the Lord Jesus. Sacrificial faithfulness to Christ in one generation reverberates for many generations to follow.

❖ **For Discussion:** Spend time discussing the implications of the Great Commission for Christians today. Whether you relocate to another country or not, what can you do to be a faithful witness for the Lord Jesus?

## II. WILLIAM CAREY (1761–1834)

Known as the "father of modern missions," Carey helped found the _____ Baptist Missionary Society. _____

Carey was a shoemaker by trade. But by studying while working, he taught himself Greek, Hebrew, and a number of other languages.

In 1781, he married Dorothy, with whom he had six children. Only three of his children survived to adulthood.

In that same year, his friend Andrew Fuller wrote a pamphlet entitled *The Gospel Worthy of All Acceptation.* This pamphlet encouraged Christians in England to think about missionary work overseas.

In 1785, Carey was also deeply impacted by Edwards's *Account of the Life of the Late Rev. David Brainerd.* As a result, he became passionately concerned about taking the gospel to parts of the world where Christ was not preached.

In 1789, Carey began to pastor a small congregation in Leicester, England.

In 1792, he published an important work entitled *An Enquiry into the Obligations of Christians to Use Means for the Conversion of the Heathen.* In this book, Carey contended that the Great Commission was for all believers. He briefly traced the history of missions, surveyed the global need for the gospel, and called for a missionary society to be formed.

The initial name of that missionary society was "The Particular Baptist Society for the Propagation of the Gospel Amongst the Heathen." It was later shortened to the Baptist Missionary Society.

Carey left for India in 1793. Initially, he managed an indigo factory while working on a Bengali translation of the New Testament.

In 1801, he became a professor of Bengali at the College of Fort William in Calcutta. The college was established to provide language training to British officers. This position enabled Carey to revise his Bengali New Testament and also start a Sanskrit translation.

Carey and his fellow missionaries established a printing press to make copies of these translations.

▶ To their dismay, a devastating fire in 1812 destroyed a number of valuable documents. They were able to save the press itself, and resumed printing efforts six months later.

▶ By the end of Carey's life, the press had printed biblical materials in dozens of languages and dialects.

In 1818, the mission established a training school for pastors, which offered education to students without respect to their place in the caste system.

Carey died on June 9, 1834, having devoted his life to the advancement of the gospel in _____India_____. He had a great influence on the cause of missions in the nineteenth century.

> ❖ **For Discussion:** One of Carey's famous sayings was "Expect great things from God; attempt great things for God." What do you think about that statement? How did it play itself out in Carey's life? What would change in your life if you adopted that kind of perspective?

## III. ADONIRAM JUDSON (1788–1850)

Adoniram Judson was born in _____Massachusetts_____ just twelve years after the United States gained independence from Britain.

- ▶ Though he grew up in a pastor's home, Judson walked away from his Christian upbringing as a college student.

- ▶ While away at university, he had been influenced by a friend named Jacob Eames, who convinced him to abandon Christianity and become a deist—essentially, a practical atheist.

- ▶ On his twentieth birthday, in August of 1808, Judson broke the news to his parents, to their great dismay. He added that he was leaving home to go to New York where he planned to work as a playwright.

- ▶ Judson claimed he was done with God. But God was not done with him.

- ▶ Sometime later, while traveling through a small town, Judson stopped for the night at an inn. As he tried to fall asleep, he heard the sound of someone dying in the next room. The thought of death made him toss and turn; he could not stop thinking about eternity.

- ▶ In the morning, as he left, he learned that the man in the next room had died. To his shock, Judson further discovered that the deceased was none other than his friend, Jacob Eames. The man who had convinced him to become a deist was now dead.

The Lord providentially used that event to bring Adoniram Judson back to Himself. Four years later, in 1812, after finishing seminary, Judson would become one of the first foreign missionaries to set out from North America.

He married his wife, Ann, on February 5, 1812; and just two weeks later, the newlyweds set sail for India.

Several months before they got married, in a moving letter to his future father-in-law, Judson spelled out the sacrifice he was asking his future bride to make. Here is part of that letter:

> **Adoniram Judson:** "I have now to ask whether you can consent to part with your daughter early next spring, to see her no more in this world; whether you can consent to her departure for a heathen land, and her subjection to the hardships and sufferings of a missionary life; whether you can consent to her exposure to the dangers of the ocean; to the fatal influence of the southern climate of India; to every kind of want and distress; to degradation, insult, persecution, and perhaps a violent death?

"Can you consent to all this for the sake of Him who left His heavenly home, and died for her and for you; for the sake of perishing immortal souls; for the sake of Zion and the glory of God? Can you consent to all this in hope of soon meeting your daughter in the world of glory, with a crown of righteousness brightened by the acclamations of praise which shall redound to her Savior from heathens saved, through her means, from eternal woe and despair?"[3]

Armed with that kind of heavenly perspective, the Judsons set sail for India.

They soon encountered economic challenges, losing the financial backing of their supporters only a few months after leaving the United States.

Then their plans unexpectedly changed when problems with their visas in India forced them to settle in Burma.

Once there, they faced a severe language barrier, requiring years of intense language study to overcome.

When they finally could communicate, their message was met with relative indifference from the people, due in part to an imperial death-sentence for anyone convicted of changing religions.

After twelve years of work, Judson and his fellow missionaries saw only eighteen conversions.

Beyond the constant threat of sickness and disease, Judson also faced serious threats from the government.

- ▶ Suspected of being a spy during Burma's civil war, he was sent to a death prison where he was tortured and forced on a death march that nearly killed him.

- ▶ In all, he spent seventeen months behind bars in harsh conditions while his wife, Ann, did everything she could to secure his release.

More painful than that, Judson endured the pain of loss some two dozen times. His wife, Ann, died just a few months after he was released from prison. She would not be the only family member who died during his tenure.

- ▶ From 1812 to 1850, two dozen of Judson's relatives or close associates went home to heaven, including several of his children.

Enduring all of this, he pursued his goal of evangelizing the Burmese people and translating the Bible into their language.

When he died, the translation work had been completed, 100 churches had been planted, and 8,000 Burmese professed faith in the Lord Jesus.

Adoniram Judson and his family made enormous sacrifices for the sake of the gospel. From a worldly perspective, some might wonder why they moved far away from the comforts of their North American roots; endured the pain of rejection, hunger, torture, and loss; and did all of this to bring good news to a largely antagonistic audience.

But Judson was motivated by a radically different outlook on life—one in which he sought to live each day for eternity.

Looking back, of course, we see that Judson's efforts were not in vain.

Nearly 150 years after Judson's death, in 1993, the head of the Myanmar Evangelical Fellowship stated, "Today, there are 6 million Christians in Myanmar, and every one of us trace our spiritual heritage to one man—the Reverend Adoniram Judson."[4]

### IV. C. T. STUDD (1860–1931)

Charles Thomas Studd was born on December 2, 1860, into a wealthy family in England. Sixteen years later, through the influence of D. L. Moody, he embraced the Lord Jesus Christ in saving faith.

He would go on to Cambridge where he would become one of the most well-known cricket players of his day, famous not only in Britain but around the world.

When his time at Cambridge ended, Charles realized that he did not want to pursue a career in athletics. As he said it,

> "What is all the fame and flattery worth . . . when a man comes to face eternity?"[5]

> "I know that cricket would not last, and honor would not last, and nothing in this world would last, but it [is] worthwhile living for the world to come."[6]

> "How could I spend the best years of my life in working for myself and the honors and pleasures of this world, when thousands and thousands of souls are perishing every day?"[7]

Armed with an eternal perspective and motivated by a desire to serve Christ no matter the cost, C. T. Studd left England to serve as a missionary in China, under the oversight of Hudson Taylor.

He spent a decade in China, much of that time working in a rehabilitation center for opium addicts, sharing the gospel and seeing lives transformed by God's grace.

- ► While in China, he married his wife, Priscilla, and together they had four daughters.

After spending a few years back in England, the family moved to India, where Charles pastored a local church for seven years.

- ► Though he struggled with severe asthma, often staying awake most of the night just trying to breathe, he faithfully preached the gospel. As a result, many souls in Southern India were won to the Lord.

Shortly thereafter, C. T. Studd became convinced that God wanted him to take the gospel to the interiors of Africa.

- ► He eventually reached the Belgian Congo in 1913, enduring various challenges and difficulties. At one point, he contracted a severe case of malaria; on another occasion, he woke up one morning to discover a venomous snake had been sleeping by his side all night long.

Along with his fellow missionaries, he established a number of missionary stations in the heart of Africa, bringing the gospel to indigenous tribal groups that had previously never heard the name of Jesus Christ.

He wrote over two hundred hymns and translated the New Testament into the native language.

C. T. Studd died in Africa, at the age of seventy, having spent almost his entire adult life in missionary service: ten years in China, seven years in India, and roughly twenty years in Africa. Through his unwavering perseverance, numerous souls were reached with the good news of the gospel.

As one might imagine, that kind of pioneering missionary work was taxing. But Studd's response was simple and sincere. He said, "If Jesus Christ be God and died for me, then no sacrifice can be too great for me to make for Him."[8]

That undying commitment to serve Christ—no matter the cost—is perhaps best captured in the words of a poem he wrote. Perhaps you've heard these words before:

> Two little lines I heard one day, Traveling along life's busy way;
> Bringing conviction to my heart, And from my mind would not depart;
> Only one life, 'twill soon be past, Only what's done for Christ will last.
>
> Only one life, yes only one, Soon will its fleeting hours be done;
> Then, in 'that day' my Lord to meet, And stand before His Judgment seat;
> Only one life, 'twill soon be past, Only what's done for Christ will last.[9]

❖ **For Discussion:** As you read the words of the poem above, what stands out to you? How do those words bring clarity to the proper priority structure for life?

## V. CONSIDERING THE CALL

Even a brief survey of the modern missions movement is compelling. Our hearts ought to be stirred by the examples of faithful men and women who sacrificed earthly comfort for the sake of heavenly gain. Through their efforts, the gospel went forth to the ends of the earth.

The power behind this global movement was the same power behind the Reformation. The Spirit of God used His Word, translated and preached, to open eyes and transform hearts. As a result, millions of people around the globe would come to believe in the Lord Jesus.

The fruit of _____salvation_____ is entirely a work of God. Yet, He uses human instruments to accomplish His saving purposes (Rom. 10:9–15).

Just prior to the birth of the church (in Acts 2), Christ commanded His followers to be His witnesses to the ends of the earth (Acts 1:8). In every generation, believers are called to be faithful to fulfill the Great Commission (Matthew 28:18–20). This lesson provides just a glimpse into all God is doing around the world.

Recognizing the need for more missionaries to be sent, the renowned British preacher Charles Spurgeon (1834–1892) urged the students at his Pastors College to consider ministering overseas. His charge to them serves as a fitting concluding challenge to us:

**Charles Spurgeon:** "I plead this day for those who cannot plead for themselves, namely, the great outlying masses of the heathen world. Our existing pulpits are tolerably well supplied, but we need men who will build on new foundations. Who will do this? Are we, as a company of faithful men, clear in our consciences about the heathen? Millions have never heard the Name of Jesus. Hundreds of millions have seen a missionary only once in their lives, and know nothing of our King. Shall we let them perish? . . . The dangers incident to missions ought not to keep any true man back, even if they were very great, but they are now reduced to a minimum. There are hundreds of places where the cross of Christ is unknown, to which we can go without risk. Who will go?"[10]

❖ **For Discussion:** Have you ever considered the possibility of missionary work overseas, whether short-term or long-term? If not, why not? If so, how did you think through that possibility?

# Lesson 13

# THE BATTLE FOR THE BIBLE
Faithful Believers in the Face of Modernism

**KEY PASSAGE: 2 Timothy 3:16–17**

*"All Scripture is inspired by God and profitable for teaching, for reproof, for correction, for training in righteousness; so that the man of God may be adequate, equipped for every good work."*

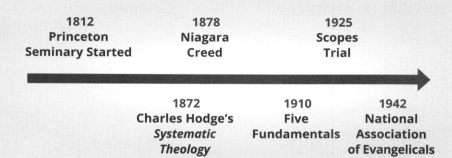

| 1812<br>Princeton<br>Seminary Started | 1878<br>Niagara<br>Creed | 1925<br>Scopes<br>Trial |
|---|---|---|
| 1872<br>Charles Hodge's<br>*Systematic Theology* | 1910<br>Five<br>Fundamentals | 1942<br>National<br>Association<br>of Evangelicals |

## I. THE BIBLE COMES UNDER ATTACK

In the seventeenth and eighteenth centuries, the philosophical underpinnings of Europe began to shift. The rise of Rationalism (which emphasized human reason) and Empiricism (which focused on the scientific method) began to replace the religious traditionalism that had been prevalent throughout the Middle Ages. This shift is known as the Enlightenment, or the Age of Reason.

At the outset, this movement was primarily led by Christian philosophers and scientists. But it soon became dominated by those who claimed the Bible should be discarded. Armed with reason and science, some Enlightenment thinkers openly questioned the inspiration, authority, and accuracy of Scripture.

These skeptics challenged the veracity of Scripture. They denied the biblical accounts of supernatural events, arguing that miracles were either legends or coincidences that could be explained as the result of natural causes.

They also denied the original authorship of many parts of Scripture. For instance, they asserted that Moses did not write the Pentateuch, and taught that the gospels were not historical accounts about the life of Jesus.

This attack on the trustworthiness of the Bible caused some professing Christians to question whether Scripture should be regarded as the foundation for the Christian faith. Some argued the basis for Christianity should be found in feelings of dependence on God; others looked to social activism and the church's influence in society.

As a result, a new category emerged in church history—the category of "liberal Christianity" or "theological liberalism." Broadly speaking, liberalism rejected the inspiration and inerrancy of Scripture, and redefined the church's mission in terms of things likes social activism.

By the early twentieth century, theological liberalism was prevalent in both Europe and the United States. In addition to rejecting (1) the inerrancy of Scripture, many proponents of liberalism also denied (2) the deity of Christ, (3) the miracles recorded in the Bible, (4) the substitutionary atonement of Jesus' death on the cross, and (5) the bodily resurrection of Christ.

In response to these attacks, Bible-believing Christians from various Protestant denominations (Baptists, Presbyterians, Methodists, and more) banded together to defend the cardinal doctrines of the Christian faith.

In the 1920s, these Christians became known as "fundamentalists," because they believed the fundamental truths of Scripture and were willing to contend earnestly for them (see Jude 3–4).

In this lesson, we will survey the ideological battle that took place in the early twentieth century, especially in the United States, between the theologically-liberal "Modernists" and the Bible-believing Fundamentalists.

❖ **For Discussion:** Look again at the key passage for this lesson (2 Tim. 3:16–17). What does the Bible claim for itself? How does that claim differ from the skeptical attacks made by theological liberals?

## II. PRINCETON THEOLOGY

As theological liberalism began to spread, in the mid-eighteenth century, the Lord raised up a formidable defense at Princeton Theological Seminary.

Princeton Seminary was started in 1812 by Archibald Alexander (1772–1851), who served as the school's first chair of systematic theology.

Notable nineteenth-century faculty members included:

▶ Charles Hodge (1797–1878) is best known for the Systematic Theology that he published in 1872. Hodge taught at Princeton for more than fifty years. During that time, he staunchly defended the Christian faith from attack.

▶ A. A. Hodge (1823–1886) was the son of Charles and was named after Princeton Seminary's first president, Archibald Alexander. He became a professor of systematic theology at Princeton Seminary when his father died in 1878. He, too, defended the doctrine of biblical inerrancy.

▶ Benjamin B. Warfield (1851–1921) succeeded A. A. Hodge as the professor of systematic theology in 1877. He was a prolific writer and an ardent defender of the fundamental doctrines of the Christian faith.

When we consider the three pillars of doctrinal orthodoxy that we have been tracing through church history, we find them clearly defended by the Princeton theologians. Consider, for example, the following quotes from B. B. Warfield.

The true church is characterized by its commitment to:

1. **The _____Word_____ of God (in Scripture):** The true church views Scripture alone as its final authority. Followers of Jesus submit to Him by submitting to His Word.

   ▶ **Warfield:** "When Paul declares, then, that 'every Scripture,' or 'all Scripture' is the product of the Divine breath, 'is God-breathed,' he asserts with as much energy as he could employ that Scripture is the product of a specifically Divine operation."[1]

   ▶ **Warfield:** "The Bible is the Word of God in such a way that when the Bible speaks, God speaks."[2]

   ▶ **Warfield:** "Thus in every way possible, the church has borne her testimony from the beginning, and still in our day, to her faith in the divine trustworthiness of her Scriptures, in all their affirmations of whatever kind. . . . The church has always believed her Scriptures to be the book of God, of which God was in such a sense the author that every one of its affirmations of whatever kind is to be esteemed as the utterance of God, of infallible truth and authority."[3]

2. **The _____work_____ of God (in salvation):** The true church understands that sinners are justified by God's grace through faith apart from works. They recognize their salvation is based entirely on the finished work of Jesus Christ, who rose bodily from the grave.

   ▶ **Warfield:** "We have but one Savior; and that one Savior is Jesus Christ our Lord. Nothing that we are and nothing that we can do enters in the slightest measure into the ground of our acceptance with God. Jesus did it all."[4]

   ▶ **Warfield:** "From the empty grave of Jesus the enemies of the cross turn away in unconcealable dismay. . . . Christ has risen from the dead! After two thousand years of the most determined assault upon the evidence which demonstrates it, that fact stands. And so long as it stands Christianity, too, must stand as the one supernatural religion."[5]

3. **The _____worship_____ of God (in spirit and truth):** The true church worships the Triune God (Father, Son, and Holy Spirit) in purity of devotion and purity of doctrine. This includes a clear affirmation of the deity of Christ.

   ▶ **Warfield:** "The deity of Christ is in solution in every page of the New Testament. Every word that is spoken of Him, every word which He is reported to have spoken of Himself, is spoken on the assumption that He is God. And that is the reason why the 'criticism' which addresses itself to eliminating the testimony of the New Testament to the deity of our Lord has set itself a hopeless task. The New Testament itself would have to be eliminated. Nor can we get behind this testimony. Because the deity of Christ is the presupposition of every word of the New Testament."[6]

   ▶ **Warfield:** "Had Christ not risen we could not believe Him to be what He declared Himself when He 'made Himself equal with God.' But He has risen in the confirmation of all His claims. By it alone, but by it thoroughly, is He manifested as the very Son of God, who has come into the world to reconcile the world to Himself. It is the fundamental fact in the Christian's unwavering confidence in 'all the words of this life.'"[7]

❖ **For Discussion:** One of the tenets of the Christian faith that Warfield defended was the historicity of Christ's resurrection. Read 1 Corinthians 15:14–20. Why is the resurrection so essential to the Christian faith?

## III. THE RISE OF FUNDAMENTALISM

The term "fundamentalist" generally has a negative connotation in contemporary culture. But as noted above, fundamentalism began as a movement consisting of _____Bible-believing_____ Christians.

In the late-nineteenth and early-twentieth centuries, this movement included well-known evangelists, like _____Dwight L. Moody_____ (1837–1899), _____C. I. Scofield_____ (1843–1921), and _____Billy Sunday_____ (1882–1935).

The movement was also associated with various Bible conferences, like the Niagara Bible Conference (which met annually from 1876–1897). In 1878, a group of scholars associated with this conference articulated fourteen doctrinal principles outlining basic Christian beliefs. These fourteen points comprised the "Niagara Creed."

Other groups created similar statements or creeds, in an effort to safeguard essential biblical doctrines in the face of liberalism's growing influence.

In 1910, the General Assembly of the Presbyterian Church identified "five fundamentals." These fundamental doctrines included:

1. _____ The inerrancy of Scripture _____

2. _____ The virgin birth and deity of Jesus Christ _____

3. _____ The substitutionary atonement of Christ's death _____

4. _____ The bodily resurrection of Christ _____

5. _____ The authenticity of Christ's miracles _____

That same year, a Presbyterian businessman named Lyman Stewart funded the publication of *The Fundamentals: A Testimony to the Truth*.

*The Fundamentals* consisted of ninety essays written by sixty-four authors from several denominations. They were published in twelve installments between 1910 and 1915.

The articles themselves expanded on the five fundamentals, and strengthened the fundamentalist stance against modernism and skeptical attacks on Scripture.

When reading *The Fundamentals*, it becomes clear that the founders of fundamentalism championed the authority of Scripture. Here are three examples:

> **The Fundamentals**: "The living Word shall continue to be the discerning companion of all who resort to it for the help which is not to be had elsewhere in this world of the dying. In going to the Bible we never think of ourselves as going back to a book of the distant past, to a thing of antiquity; but we go to it as to a book of the present—a living book. And so indeed it is, living in the power of an endless life, and able to build us up and to give us an inheritance among all them that are sanctified."[8]

> **The Fundamentals**: "Luther said that he studied the Bible as he gathered apples. First, he shook the whole tree, that the ripest might fall. Then he climbed the tree and shook each limb, and when he had shaken each limb, he shook each branch, and after each branch every twig, and then looked under each leaf. Let us search the Bible as a whole; shake the whole tree; read it as rapidly as you would any other book; then shake every limb, studying book after book. Then shake every branch, giving attention to the chapters when they do not break the sense. Then shake every twig by careful study of the paragraphs and sentences, and you will be rewarded, if you will look under every leaf, by searching the meaning of words."[9]

> **The Fundamentals**: "We know not the day nor the hour when the Lord will come, or call us hence; and we want to be ready, both as to purity of character and the courtly culture of the heavenly city. We wish to be familiar with the history of redemption, and with the mysteries of the kingdom. We should not want to appear as an awkward stranger in our Father's house of light. We can only get this sanctification of character and culture of life and manner by constant familiarity and communion with God and the saints through the Word…. The Word of God is a chart that marks all the rocks and reefs in the sea of life; if we heed, and sail our frail bark by it, we shall come safely into the haven of rest."[10]

Those who embraced the five fundamentals, and who were willing to fight for those doctrinal truths, came to be known as "Fundamentalists."

Curtis Lee Laws is credited with first using the term. He was the editor of *The Watchman Examiner*, and in the July 1, 1920 issue, he wrote: "We suggest that those who still cling to the great fundamentals and who mean to do battle royal for the fundamentals shall be called 'Fundamentalists.'"

## IV. FUNDAMENTALISM VS. MODERNISM

In the early 1900s, an ideological battle was fought within the mainline American denominations between Bible-believing Christians and theological liberals. This is known as the "Fundamentalist-Modernist" controversy.

That controversy was especially heated in Presbyterian circles. The conflict began to brew when several Presbyterian seminary professors were removed because they denied the doctrine of biblical inerrancy.

In 1922, Harry Emerson Fosdick, a liberal Baptist minister, preached a sermon at the First Presbyterian Church New York entitled, "Shall the Fundamentalists Win?" He adamantly insisted they should not.

Fourteen years later, in 1936, J. Gresham Machen (1881–1937) left the Presbyterian Church USA (PCUSA) to establish the Orthodox Presbyterian Church (OPC). Machen was one of the last theological conservatives to teach at Princeton Seminary. When Princeton grew increasingly favorable towards liberalism, Machen left.

This controversy within Presbyterian circles was representative of what was happening in all of American Christianity. As a result of these struggles, American Protestantism was split into "mainline Protestants" on the one hand and "fundamentalists" on the other.

Public opinion against fundamentalism increased as a result of the Scopes Monkey Trial of 1925.

▶ John T. Scopes (a substitute high school biology teacher in Tennessee) was accused of teaching the theory of evolution in a public school, which violated Tennessee state law.

▶ The prosecution was led by William Jennings Bryan, a three-time presidential candidate. The defense attorney, Clarence Darrow, was also well-known, which brought national attention to the trial.

▶ Although Scopes was found guilty, the trial itself generated negative publicity for fundamentalists (and their creationist views)—which were perceived to be outdated and contrary to scientific progress.

Sadly, in both the mainline denominations and the court of public opinion, fundamentalism began to lose support. It seemed as if Bible-believing Christians were being marginalized in American society.

In leaving the mainline denominations, fundamentalists started new organizations such as the Orthodox Presbyterian Church (OPC), the Presbyterian Church in America (PCA), the Conservative Baptist Association of America (CBAmerica), and the General Association of Regular Baptist Churches (GARBC).

## V. THE RISE OF NEW EVANGELICALISM

In the 1940s, a group of Bible-believing Christians sought to distance themselves from fundamentalism. In particular, they were concerned that the fundamentalist movement had become known for infighting and anti-intellectualism.

This group began to identify themselves as "New Evangelicals," or later simply as "Evangelicals." In 1942, they established an organization called the _____ National Association of Evangelicals. _____

These early evangelicals openly affirmed their belief in the inspiration and inerrancy of the Bible, the deity of Christ, His atoning death on the cross, and His bodily resurrection from the grave. However, they insisted their tone needed to be more friendly than that of earlier fundamentalists.

In the 1950s and 60s, a preacher named Billy Graham (1918–2018) emerged as a popular evangelist. Though Graham grew up in fundamentalist circles, his willingness to partner with theological liberals and Roman Catholics in his evangelistic crusades caused many fundamentalists to separate from Graham. By contrast, many American evangelicals viewed Graham as a spokesman for their movement.

In the 1970s and 80s, evangelicals became increasingly engaged in American politics. As a result, the evangelical movement in the United States is often associated with certain political platforms. This can be confusing both for those outside and inside evangelicalism.

The term _____ *evangelical* _____ comes from the Greek word for _____ "gospel". _____ If evangelicals are to be true to both their name and their heritage, they must not forget to focus on the accurate and bold proclamation of the good news of Jesus Christ.

In their quest for influence, evangelicals have sometimes compromised their fidelity to biblical truth. Too often, success is measured in terms of numbers or popularity rather than in terms of faithfulness to God.

At the same time, we can be grateful for the many churches, across the world, that have been faithful to honor God's Word and contend earnestly for the faith. They have embraced their evangelical heritage in its truest sense, defending the truth as they proclaim the gospel of Jesus Christ to a world in need.

❖ **For Discussion:** What comes to mind when you hear the term *evangelical*? Given that it comes from the Greek word for "gospel" or "good news," how should evangelicalism be defined?

## VI. STANDING FIRM IN THIS GENERATION

If evangelicals are to stand firm in this generation, they must ground their convictions in the doctrinal pillars articulated by the New Testament.

▶ First, we must hold fast to the authority of God's Word without wavering. The Reformer's commitment to "Scripture alone" should be our commitment as well.

Holding to doctrines like the inspiration, inerrancy, and sufficiency of Scripture may make us unpopular.

But if our goal is *faithfulness*, the choice between honoring God and pleasing men is a clear one to make (Acts 5:29).

This lesson is titled "The Battle for the Bible." Historic fundamentalism contended earnestly for the truth of Scripture, in the face of liberal attack.

Evangelicalism's heritage—going back to the Reformation and earlier—is similarly rooted in a commitment to the authority and sufficiency of God's Word.

If we are to be faithful, we must similarly take our stand on the truth of God's Word.

► Second, we must contend for the purity of the gospel. Sinners are saved by grace alone through faith alone based on the finished work of Christ alone.

   Our love for Christ should motivate our witness to the world.

   At times, our commitment to the truth of the gospel will mean we cannot condone or partner with groups or movements that distort the gospel (Gal. 1:6–9).

   Gospel clarity is what the world around us desperately needs. In an age when we are told that truth is relative, and all belief systems are equally valid, it requires gospel courage to proclaim the exclusive message of salvation through Jesus Christ. But that is the very message people need to hear.

   **Acts 4:12**—"And there is salvation in no one else; for there is no other name under heaven that has been given among men by which we must be saved."

► Finally, we ought to do all of this as an act of worship for the glory of God alone.

   Doctrinally, we look to God's Word to understand who He is, so that we can worship Him accurately.

   The truth of Scripture ought to govern both our private devotion and our corporate worship. Accordingly, churches should look to God's Word in determining how they conduct their services—rather than giving in to entertainment-driven trends. As noted above, *faithfulness* must be the goal, not popularity.

   Morally, we seek to obey His commandments out of love for Him. We want our entire lives to be an act of acceptable worship (Rom. 12:1–2).

As we discussed in Lesson 1, we desire to be characterized by a right understanding of the Word of God, the work of God, and the worship of God.

Armed with biblical convictions, we can stand firm in this generation of church history. We recognize the strength to do this does not originate in us. It is found in Christ.

He is both the Lord of the church and the Lord of history. To Him be the glory forever and ever. Amen.

❖ **For Discussion:** How can Christians stand firm in this generation? What is one lesson you have learned from your study of church history?

# NOTES

## INTRODUCTION

1. This section is adapted from a chapter in *Right Thinking in a Church Gone Astray*, © 2017 by Nathan Busenitz. Published by Harvest House Publishers, Eugene, Oregon 97408. www.harvesthousepublishers. com. Used by permission.

## LESSON 1

1. For more on this topic, see Nathan Busenitz, "The Ground and Pillar of the Faith: The Witness of Pre-Reformation History to the Doctrine of *Sola Scriptura*," in *The Inerrant Word*, ed. John MacArthur (Wheaton, IL: Crossway, 2016).

2. Irenaeus, *Against Heresies*, 3.1.1. Trans. from *Ante-Nicene Fathers*, eds. Alexander Roberts and James Donaldson, 10 vols. (Reprint, Peabody, MA: Hendrickson, 1994), 1:414. Hereafter *ANF*.

3. Basil, *On the Holy Spirit*, 66. Trans. from *Nicene and Post-Nicene Fathers*, Second Series, eds. Philip Schaff and Henry Wace, 14 vols. (Reprint, Peabody, MA: Hendrickson, 1994), 8:229. Hereafter *NPNF2*.

## LESSON 3

1. Clement, *First Clement*, 32:4. Trans. from Michael W. Holmes, *The Apostolic Fathers: Greek Texts and English Translations*, 3rd ed. (Grand Rapids: Baker Academic, 2007), 87. Hereafter, *AF*. Note that divine pronouns have been capitalized to maintain formatting consistency. Also see *ANF*, 1:13.

2. Ignatius, *Epistle to the Magnesians*, 9. Trans. from *ANF* 1:62.

3. See Bruce Shelley, *Church History in Plain Language*, 3rd ed. (Nashville: Thomas Nelson, 2008), 70.

4. Polycarp, *Epistle to the Philippians*, 1. Trans. from *AF* 281. See *ANF* 1:33.

5. Polycarp, *Epistle to the Philippians*, 2.1. Trans. from *AF* 283. See *ANF* 1:33.

6. Polycarp, *Epistle to the Philippians*, 6.3. Trans. from *AF* 289. See *ANF* 1:34.

7. Polycarp, *Epistle to the Philippians*, 8.1–2. Trans. from *AF* 289–91. See *ANF* 1:35.

8. Polycarp, *Epistle to the Philippians,* 10.1. Trans. from *AF* 291. See *ANF* 1:35.

9. *The Martyrdom of Polycarp*, 9. Trans. from *ANF* 1:41.

10. *The Martyrdom of Polycarp*, 19. Trans. from *ANF* 1:43.

11. *The Didache*, 1.1–2. Trans. from *AF* 345.

12. *The Didache*, 2.1–2. Trans. from *AF* 347.

13. *Epistle to Diognetus*, 9.2–6. Trans. from *ANF* 1:28.

**LESSON 4**

1. Justin, *First Apology*, 67. Trans. from *ANF* 1:186.

2. Irenaeus, *Against Heresies*, 3.1.1. Trans. from *ANF* 1:414.

3. Irenaeus, *Against Heresies*, 3.4.1–2. Trans. from *ANF* 1:417.

4. Tertullian, *Prescription Against Heresies*, 7. Trans. from *ANF* 3:246.

**LESSON 5**

1. Gregory of Nyssa, *On the Holy Trinity, and of the Godhead of the Holy Spirit*. Trans. from *NPNF2* 5:327.

2. Pliny, *Letters*, 10.96–97. Letter to the Emperor Trajan.

3. Ignatius, *Letter to the Ephesians*, 18.2. Trans. from *AF* 197. See also *Letter to the Ephesians*, 19.3; Ignatius, *Letter to the Romans*, 3.3; Ignatius, *Letter to the Smyrnaeans*, 1.1. In finding a number of the patristic citations in this section, I am indebted to John Ankerberg and John Weldon, *Knowing the Truth about the Trinity* (Chattanooga, TN: ATRI Publishing, 2011).

4. Ignatius, *Letter to Polycarp*, 3.2. Trans. from *AF* 265.

5. Polycarp, *Philippians* 12:2. Trans. from *AF* 295.

6. *Epistle of Barnabas*, 5.5. Trans. from *AF* 393.

7. Justin Martyr, *Dialogue with Trypho*, 36. Trans. from *ANF* 1:212.

8. Justin Martyr, *Dialogue with Trypho*, 63; *ANF* 229. See also Justin Martyr, *First Apology*, 63; Justin Martyr, *Dialogue with Trypho*, 126.

9. Tatian, *Address to the Greeks*, 21. Trans. from *ANF* 2:74.

10. Melito, *Fragments*, 5. Trans. from *ANF* 8:757.

11. Irenaeus, *Against Heresies*, 3.19.2. Trans. from *ANF* 1:449.

12. Irenaeus, *Against Heresies*, 1.10.1. Trans. from *ANF* 1:330.

13. Irenaeus, *Against Heresies*, 4.5.2. Trans. from *ANF* 1:467.

14. Irenaeus, *Against Heresies*, 4.6.7. Trans. from *ANF* 1:469.

15. Clement of Alexandria, *Exhortation to the Heathen*, 1. Trans. from *ANF* 2:173.

16. Tertullian, *Treatise on the Soul*, 41. Trans. from *ANF* 3:221.

17. Tertullian, *Apology*, 21. Trans. from *ANF* 3:34–35.

18. Caius, *Fragments*, 2.1. Trans. from *ANF* 5:601.

19. The Nicene Creed. Trans. adapted from Stephen Nichols, *For Us and For Our Salvation* (Wheaton, IL: Crossway, 2007), 96.

**LESSON 6**

1. Augustine, *The Spirit and the Letter*, 13 (22). *PL* 44.214–15. Trans. from *Nicene and Post-Nicene Fathers*, First Series, ed. Philip Schaff, 14 vol. (Reprint, Peabody, MA: Hendrickson, 1994), 5:93. Hereafter, *NPNF1*.

2. Augustine, *To Simplician—On Various Questions*, 1.2.5. Trans. from Burleigh, *Augustine: Earlier Writings* (Louisville: Westminster John Knox, 1953), 389. See also Augustine, *Epistle 194.3.7*.

3. Augustine, *Exp. prop. Rom.* 20. Trans. from Oden, *The Justification Reader* (Grand Rapids: Eerdmans, 2002), 145.

4. Augustine, *C. du. ep. Pelag.* 1.21.39. Trans. from Elowsky, W*e Believe in the Holy Spirit* (Downers Grove, IL: InterVarsity Press, 2009), 96.

5. Augustine, *Enarrat. Ps.*, 31.7. Trans. from John E. Rotelle, *Expositions of the Psalms 1–32* (Hyde Park: New City Press, 2000), 11.370.

6. Augustine, *Enarrat. Ps.*, 55.12 [56.11]. Trans. from *NPNF1* 8:222. English updated for clarity.

7. Augustine, *Letters*, 214.3. Trans. from Bray, *1–2 Corinthians*, Ancient Christian Commentary on Scripture: New Testament (Downers Grove, IL: InterVarsity, 1999), 39. Cf. Augustine, *Letters 204–270*, Fathers of the Church, trans. Wilfrid Parsons (Washington, DC: The Catholic University of America Press, 1981), 60.

8. Augustine, *Letters,* 214.4. Trans. from *NPNF1* 5:438. See also Augustine, *Gest. Pelag.* 14.34.

9. For an extended discussion on this point, see Nathan Busenitz, *Long before Luther* (Chicago: Moody, 2017).

10. Augustine, *Letters*, 82.3. For a more detailed discussion of patristic quotes related to Scripture, see William Webster, *Holy Scripture: The Ground and Pillar of Our Faith*, vol. 2 (Battle Ground, WA: Christian Resources, 2001).

11. Augustine, *Sermons* 23.3. Trans. from Peter Gorday, ed., *Colossians, 1–2 Thessalonians, 1–2 Timothy, Titus, Philemon.* Ancient Christian Commentary on Scripture: New Testament. (Downers Grove, IL: InterVarsity Press, 2000), comment on 2 Tim. 3:16.

12. Augustine, *Letters,* 28.3, to Jerome. Trans. from *NPNF2* 1:251–252.

13. Augustine, *The City of God*, 11.3. Trans. from *NPNF1* 2.206.

14. Augustine, *The City of God*, 21.6.1.

15. For example, Augustine writes, "For the reasonings of any men whatsoever, even though they be [Christians], and of high reputation, are not to be treated by us in the same way as the canonical Scriptures are treated. We are at liberty, without doing any violence to the respect which these men deserve, to condemn and reject anything in their writings, if perchance we shall find that they have entertained opinions differing from that which others or we ourselves have, by the divine help, discovered to be the truth. I deal thus with the writings of others, and I wish my intelligent readers to deal thus with mine." Augustine, *Letters*, 148.15.

16. Augustine, *Reply to Faustus*, 11.5.

17. Augustine, *The Unity of the Church*, 3; cited from Martin Chemnitz, *Examination of the Council of Trent*, 4 vols., trans. Fred Kramer (St. Louis: Concordia, 1971), 1.157.

18. Augustine, *The Unity of the Church*, 3; as cited by Chemnitz, *Examination of the Council of Trent*, 1.157.

19. Augustine, *Contra Maximin. Arian.* 2.14. Trans. from *NPNF1* 8.704. See also George Salmon, *The Infallibility of the Church* (Grand Rapids: Baker Book House, 1959), 295.

20. Augustine, *On Christian Doctrine*, 2.9.

21. Augustine, *On the Good of Widowhood*, 2. Trans. from *NPNF1* 3.442.

22. John Chrysostom, *Hom. Rom.* 7 (on Rom. 3:27). Trans. from *NPNF1* 11.379.

23. John Chrysostom, *Hom. Rom.* 9 (on Rom. 5:2). Trans. from *NPNF1* 11.396. English updated slightly.

24. John Chrysostom, *Hom. Eph.* (on Eph. 2:8). Trans. from Oden, *The Justification Reader*, 44.

25. John Chrysostom, *Hom. Col.* 5 (on Col. 1:26–28). Trans. from Elowsky, *We Believe in the Holy Spirit*, 98. Cf. *NPNF*[1] 13.280.

26. John Chrysostom, *Hom. 1 Tim.* (on 1 Tim. 1:15–16). Trans. from Elowsky, *We Believe in the Holy Spirit*, 98.

27. John Chrysostom, Homily on John 17:17. Trans. from Elowsky, *John 11–21*, Ancient Christian Commentary on Scripture, 252.

28. Chrysostom, *Concerning the Statutes*, Homily 1.14.

29. Chrysostom, *2 Timothy*, Homily 9.

30. Chrysostom, *Against Marcionists and Manichaens*, 1.

**LESSON 7**

1. The Nicene Creed. Trans. adapted from Nichols, *For Us and For Our Salvation*, 96.

2. Excerpt from the Expanded Nicene Creed. Trans. adapted from Thomas Richey, *The Nicene Creed and the Filioque* (New York: E. & J. B. Young, 1884), 33.

3. The Chalcedonian Creed. Trans. adapted from *The Catechism of the Catholic Church*, Second Edition (New York: Doubleday, 2012), 467. For more on Chalcedon, see Richard Price and Mary Whiby, *Chalcedon in Context* (Liverpool: University of Liverpool, 2009).

**LESSON 8**

1. Anselm, *Cur Deus hom.*, 2.21. *PL* 158.430. Trans. from Janet Fairweather. In *Anselm of Canterbury: The Major Works*, edited by Brian Davies and G. R. Evans (Oxford: Oxford University Press, 1998), 354.

2. Anselm, *Meditatio 9. PL* 158.757. Trans. from *Meditations and Prayers to the Holy Trinity and our Lord Jesus Christ*, translated by E. P. B. (Oxford: John Henry Parker, 1856, 83–84). English updated for clarity.

3. Anselm, *Meditatio 9. PL* 158.865. Trans. from *Meditations and Prayers*, 187–88. English updated for clarity.

4. Attributed to Anselm of Canterbury, *Admon. mor. PL* 158:686–687. Trans. from *Meditations and Prayers*, 275–77. English updated for clarity. Even if not from Anselm directly, this exchange illustrates the heart of a twelfth- or thirteenth-century Christian author.

5. Bernard of Clairvaux, *Fest. omn. sanct.* 1.11. *PL* 183.459. Trans. from George Stanley Faber, *The Primitive Doctrine of Justification Investigated,* 2nd ed. (London: Seely and Burnside, 1839), 185.

6. Bernard of Clairvaux, *Serm. Cant.* 50.2. *PL* 183.1021. Trans. from *Honey and Salt: Selected Spiritual Writings of Saint Bernard of Clairvaux,* ed. John F. Thornton and Susan B. Varenne (New York: Random House, 2007), 170.

7. Bernard of Clairvaux, *Serm. Cant.* 2.8. *PL* 183.793. Trans. adapted from Pedersen, "The Significance of the *Sola Fide* and the *Sola Gratia* in the Theologies of Bernard of Clairvaux (1090–1153) and Martin Luther (1483–1546)," online at: https://web.augsburg.edu/~mcguire/EMWPedersen_Bernard_Luther.pdf (accessed February 27, 2020).11.

8. Bernard of Clairvaux, *Epist.* 190.6. *PL* 182.1065. Trans. from John Mabillon, ed., *Life and Works of Saint Bernard, Abbot of Clairvaux,* trans. Samuel J. Eales (London: John Hodges, 1889), 2:580–581.

9. Bernard of Clairvaux, *Serm. Cant.* 22.8. *PL* 183.881. Trans. adapted from Franz Posset, *Pater Bernhardus: Martin Luther and Bernard of Clairvaux* (Collegeville, MN: Cistercian Publications, 2000), 186.

10. Bernard as recorded by William of St. Thierry, *S. Bern. vit. prim.* 1.12. *PL* 185.258. Trans. from Alban Butler, *The Lives of the Fathers, Martyrs, and Other Principal Saints,* vol. 8 (Dublin: James Duffy, 1845), 231. English updated for clarity.

**LESSON 9**

1. John Wycliffe, *Truth and Meaning of Scripture,* cited from *Life and Times of John Wycliffe* (London: Religious Tract Society, 1884), 116–117.

2. John Wycliffe, *Truth and Meaning of Scripture,* cited from *Life and Times of John Wycliffe,* 129–130.

3. John Wycliffe, *Truth and Meaning of Scripture,* cited from *Life and Times of John Wycliffe,* 117.

4. John Wycliffe, *How the Office of Curates Is Ordained by God,* 28; cited from *Writings of the Reverend and Learned John Wycliffe* (London: Gospel Tract Society, 1831), 185.

5. John Wycliffe, *Antichrist's Labour to Destroy Holy Writ,* 1; cited from *Writings of John Wycliffe,* 172.

6. John Wycliffe, *Wicket,* cited from *Writings of John Wycliffe,* 156.

7. John Wycliffe, *Saints Day Sermon;* cited from *Life and Times of John Wycliffe,* 142.

8. Jan Hus, cited from *550 Years of Jan Hus' Witness* (World Alliance of Reformed Churches, 1965), 1–2.

9. Jan Hus, *De Ecllesia,* cited from Matthew Spinka, *John Hus' Concept of the Church* (Princeton, NJ: Princeton University Press, 1966), 121.

10. Jan Hus, cited from "John Huss," *Christianity Today,* online at: https://www.christianitytoday.com/history/people/martyrs/john-huss.html.

11. Miles J. Standford and William B. Forbush, eds. *Foxe's Book of Martyrs* (Grand Rapids: Zondervan, 1967), 143. See also David S. Schaff, *John Huss after Five Hundred Years: His Life, Teachings, and Death* (New York: Charles Scribner's Sons, 1915), 19.

**LESSON 10**

1. Martin Luther, cited from Larry Stone, *The Story of the Bible* (Nashville: Thomas Nelson, 2010), 65.

2. Martin Luther, cited from J. H. Merle D'Aubigne, *History Of The Reformation Of The Sixteenth Century* (New York: Robert Carter and Brothers, 1850), 185.

3. Martin Luther, "Lectures on Galatians, 1535," in *Luther's Works*, vol. 26, trans. Jaroslav Pelikan (St. Louis: Concordia, 1963), 57–58.

4. *Geneva Confession of 1536*, 1. Trans. Arthur C. Cochrane, ed., *Reformed Confessions of the Sixteenth Century* (Louisville: Westminster John Knox Press, 2003), 120.

5. Martin Luther, quotation adapted from the translation by Bard Thompson, *Humanists and Reformers: A History of the Renaissance and Reformation* (Grand Rapids: Eerdmans, 1996), 388.

6. Martin Luther, cited in James M. Kittelson and Hans H. Wiersma, *Luther the Reformer* (Minneapolis: Fortress Press, 2016), 96.

7. Martin Luther, trans. from Roland Bainton, *Here I Stand* (Nashville: Abingdon Press, 2013), 182.

8. Martin Luther, "Two Kinds of Righteousness," in *Martin Luther's Basic Theological Writings* (Minneapolis: Fortress, 1989), 156–158. Cited from William Webster, *The Gospel of the Reformation* (Battle Ground, WA: Christian Resources, 1997), 72–73.

9. Martin Luther, *Commentary on Galatians*, trans. Erasmus Middleton, ed. John Prince Fallowes (Grand Rapids: Kregel, 1979), 172. English updated for clarity.

10. Calvin, *Institutes of the Christian Religion*, 1559 ed., Library of Christian Classics 20–21, ed. by John T. McNeil, trans. by Ford Lewis Battles, 2 vols. (Philadelphia: The Westminster Press, 1960), 1:726–27.

11. John Calvin, *Institutes of the Christian Religion*, 3.11.23. Battles, 1:753.

12. John Calvin, *A Little Book on the Christian Life*, trans. and eds. Aaron Clay Denlinger and Burk Parsons (Orlando, FL: Reformation Trust, 2017), 11.

13. John Calvin, *Institutes of the Christian Religion*, Battles, 1:13.

14. John Calvin, *Institutes of the Christian Religion*, Battles, 1:41.

**LESSON 11**

1. To read all of Edwards's *Resolutions*, see Jonathan Edwards, *Jonathan Edwards' Resolutions and Advice to Young Converts*, ed. Stephen J. Nichols (Phillipsburg, NJ: P&R Publishing, 2001).

**LESSON 12**

1. Anthony Norris Groves, *Journal of a Residence at Bagdad: During the Years 1830 and 1831* (London: James Nisbet, 1832), 228.

2. Elisabeth Elliot in *World Christian: Today's Missions Magazine*, vol. 7 (1988), 29.

3. Adoniram Judson, cited from *The Missionary Review of the World*, vol. 13, eds. J. M. Sherwood and A. T. Pierson (New York: Funk & Wagnals, 1890), 562.

4. Paul Borthwick, "Adoniram Judson: Endurance Personified." Cited by Jonathan McRostie, "Comfort," *Linking Together*, n.d. *Linking Together* is the newsletter of Operation Mobilization's World Partners.

5. C. T. Studd, cited from *C. T. Studd: Cricketer and Pioneer*, by Norman Grubb (Cambridge: Lutterworth Press, 2014), 33.

6. Ibid.

7. Ibid., 35.

8. Ibid., 132.

9. Poem by C. T. Studd.

10. Charles H. Spurgeon, "Forward!" in *An All-Around Ministry* (Carlisle, PA: Banner of Truth, 2000), 55–57.

**LESSON 13**

1. B. B. Warfield, *The Inspiration and Authority of the Bible* (Phillipsburg, NJ: P&R, 1990), 133.

2. B. B. Warfield, Cited in Roy B. Zuck, *Basic Bible Interpretation* (Colorado Springs, CO: David C. Cook, 2002), 7.

3. B. B. Warfield, "The Inspiration of the Bible," 614–640, *Bibliotheca Sacra* 51/104 (October 1894), 621.

4. Benjamin B. Warfield, *The Power of God Unto Salvation* (Philadelphia: Presbyterian Board of Education, 1903), 49.

5. Benjamin B. Warfield, "Christianity and the Resurrection of Christ," in *The Bible Student and Teacher: January to June 1908*, vol. 8 (New York: American Bible League, 1908), 282.

6. B. B. Warfield, "The Deity of Christ," in *The Fundamentals: A Testimony to the Truth*, ed. R. A. Torrey, A. C. Dixon, et al. (Los Angeles: Bible Institute of Los Angeles, 1917), 2:239–46.

7. B. B. Warfield, "The Resurrection of Christ a Fundamental Doctrine," 281–298, in *The Homiletic Review* 32/4 (October 1896), 296.

8. Philip Mauro, "Life in the Word," *The Fundamentals*, 2:168.

9. A. C. Dixon, "The Scriptures," *The Fundamentals*, 4:270–271.

10. George Pentecost, "What the Bible Contains for the Believer," *The Fundamentals*, 4:278–79, 84.

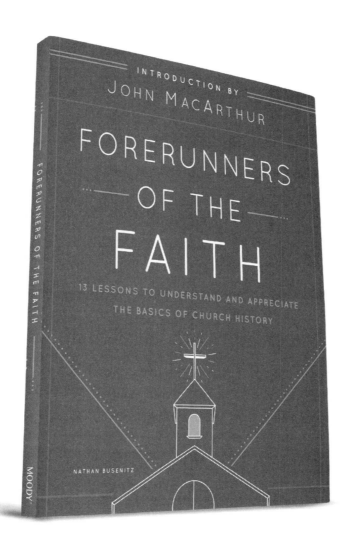

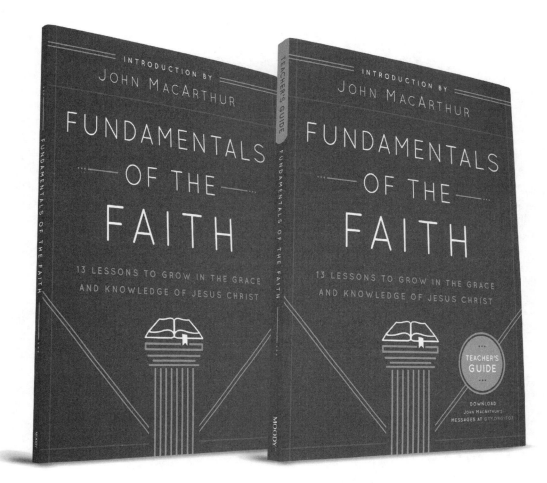

# WHERE WAS THE GOSPEL BEFORE THE REFORMATION?

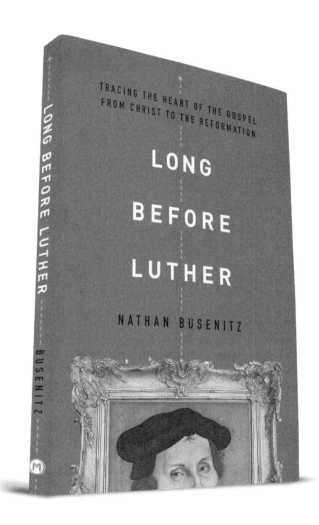

If an evangelical understanding of the gospel only traces back to the Reformation, we are in major trouble. However, if it can be demonstrated that Reformers were not inventing something new, but instead were recovering something old, then key tenets of the Protestant faith are greatly affirmed. *Long Before Luther* demonstrates that this is the case.

978-0-8024-1802-9 | also available as an eBook

# DIG DEEP INTO THE
# WHOLE NEW TESTAMENT!

## MACARTHUR NEW TESTAMENT COMMENTARY SERIES

**The set includes:**

| | | |
|---|---|---|
| Matthew (4 volumes) | Galatians | Hebrews |
| Mark (2 volumes) | Ephesians | James |
| Luke (4 volumes) | Philippians | 1 Peter |
| John (2 volumes) | Colossians & Philemon | 2 Peter and Jude |
| Acts (2 volumes) | 1 & 2 Thessalonians | 1–3 John |
| Romans (2 volumes) | 1 Timothy | Revelation (2 volumes) |
| 1 Corinthians | 2 Timothy | Index |
| 2 Corinthians | Titus | |

**MOODY
Publishers®**

*From the Word to Life®*

This bestselling 34-volume hardcover commentary set features verse-by-verse interpretation and rich application of God's Word. Easy to understand, yet rich in scholarly background.

978-0-8024-1347-5  |  also available as an eBook